Victim of Grace offers hope from first page to last! Robin Jones Gunn opens her heart and opens God's Word, sharing her fears and doubts, her plans and dreams, and how the Lord meets our needs at every turn. If you've read her novels, you know what a fine storyteller Robin is. Here she deftly weaves her own journey with scenes from the lives of biblical women we love: Hannah, Eve, Sarah, Rebekah, Hagar, Martha, Rachel, Leah. Mary Magdalene, Ruth, and Mary. A wonderful book of encouragement for women of all ages. I loved it!

—LIZ CURTIS HIGGS, bestselling author of *The Girl's Still Got It*

I love this book! Robin has dug deep into her own life experiences and allowed us to learn from them. From the opening story in chapter 1 right through the emotional ending of the last chapter she held my attention and drew heavily on my emotions. Her oft repeated comment "Everything is redeemable" resonated with me. Her candor on being open and vulnerable blessed me. Her retelling of familiar stories of Bible women revealed her personal depth as a follower of Christ. I recommend this to all who want to experience God's amazing grace.

—ROLF GARBORG, author of *The Family Blessing*

Robin Jones Gunn's life reads like a God-haunted adventure—all the ache and beauty we'd expect to see on the pages of her life. Her story is honest, unflinching and hopeful. When I closed the book, I wanted to know Jesus more and love Him more fully.

—MARY DEMUTH, author of *Everything: What You Give and What You Gain to Become Like Jesus*

I love this book. It has all the heart and intelligence you'd expect from Gunn, but with one extra bonus … the wisdom and insight of a Godly woman who has walked intimately with her Lord for decades.

—BILL MYERS, bestselling author of *Eli*

Sometimes, when I read about God doing seemingly impossible things in someone's life, I feel tempted to shrug my shoulders. "They must have a 'hot line' to heaven," I mutter. "That kind of thing just doesn't happen to most people!" Robin Jones Gunn would disagree. In her new book *Victim of Grace*, she shows us the dark valleys she has stumbled through, as well as the mountain tops on which she has danced, assuring us that the extravagant kindness and love of God isn't limited to the saints of the Bible or so-called superstars of today. He wants to make us all 'victims of His Grace.'

—Marion Stroud, author of *Dear God It's Me and It's Urgent* and *It's Just You and Me Lord*

Robin Jones Gunn has opened her life and her heart in this refreshing tale of God's grace. So often we feel caught up in life's circumstances but through her openness and generosity Robin reveals that beneath it all God is in control and if we are a victim then we are a victim of His grace.

—Debbie Macomber, *New York Times* bestselling author

I love this book! Simply poetic yet beautifully profound, Robin Jones Gunn's stories will unlock hidden places in your heart and renew your soul. This is the book I always knew my friend would write—*should* write. I didn't want it to end.

—Joanna Weaver, author of *Having a Mary Heart in a Martha World*

Robin could publish her grocery list and I would look forward to reading it! Whatever she writes comes to life and inspires me. I love her heart, I love her fiction, and I love this new book. By revealing her own heart in this book, she invites me to reveal my heart to God and receive His grace as my comfort.

—Jennifer Rothschild, author of *Lessons I Learned in the Dark*, *Self Talk, Soul Talk*, and *Missing Pieces: Real Hope When Life Doesn't Make Sense*, founder of Fresh Grounded Faith events and womensministry.net

Victim of GRACE

When God's Goodness Prevails

Robin Jones Gunn

ZONDERVAN.com/
AUTHORTRACKER
follow your favorite authors

We want to hear from you. Please send your comments about this book to us in care of zreview@zondervan.com. Thank you.

ZONDERVAN

Victim of Grace

This title is also available as a Zondervan ebook. Visit *www.zondervan.com/ebooks*.

This title is also available in a Zondervan audio edition. Visit *www.zondervan.fm*.

Requests for information should be addressed to:

Zondervan, Grand Rapids, Michigan 49530

Library of Congress Cataloging-in-Publication Data

Gunn, Robin Jones, 1955-
Victim of grace : when God's love prevails / Robin Jones Gunn.
p. cm.
Includes bibliographical references and index.
ISBN 978-0-310-32479-9 (softcover)
1. Providence and government of God—Christianity. 2. Hidden God. 3. Grace (Theology)
I. Title.
BT135.G86 2013
231.7—dc23 2012030899

Published in association with Books & Such Literary Agency, 52 Mission Circle, Suite 122, PMB 170, Santa Rosa, CA 95409-5370, www.booksandsuch.biz

Cover photography: iStockphoto®
Interior illustration: iStockphoto®
Interior design: Katherine Lloyd, The DESK

Printed in the United States of America

---

13 14 15 16 17 18 /DCI/ 26 25 24 23 22 21 20 19 18 17 16 15 14 13 12 11 10 9 8 7 6 5 4 3 2 1

For my mother

With heartfelt gratitude to
Moe, Sue, Janet, and Rachel,
who saw this book before it was formed
and believed these stories needed to be told.

For from his fullness we have all received,
grace upon grace.

—John 1:16 ESV

CONTENTS

Why does this keep happening to me?
It's not fair. I never asked to be treated this way.
I did nothing to deserve this.
And yet
Every moment of every day, completely unprovoked,
God pours out His love on me
He blesses me in unexpected ways
His mercies are new every morning.
No matter what I do I am powerless to stop Him.
Even in the worst situations His goodness prevails. He is relentless.
I am a victim of grace.

—Robin Jones Gunn

Chapter 1

FREE FALL TO FULL CIRCLE

The Lord *will fulfill his purpose for me.*

—Psalm 138:8 ESV

On a quiet summer afternoon, I handed my friend Steph a glass of iced tea and offered a sympathetic smile before taking a seat beside her on the white wicker patio chair. A rousing Maui trade wind skimmed over us and rustled the outstretched limbs of our backyard plumeria tree. A single flower on the highest branch surrendered to the tug of the unseen breeze. Nudged by another breath, the flower fluttered to the ground with airy elegance.

"Waiting is the hardest part," Steph said. "It's been eleven days and still no word. I'm stuck. I don't know if we should plan a move back to the mainland or if I should start buying school supplies since classes here start next week."

I didn't know what to tell her. I'd been in similar situations more than once in my life and I felt her frustration. No winning words of encouragement came to me.

"It's beginning to feel like a test," she said. "As if God wants to see if I completely trust him no matter what. I wish he would tell me the answer but …"

I finished the sentence for her with a line that was familiar to both of us. "But the teacher is always silent during the test."

"Exactly."

I released the thin pineapple wedge that balanced on the side of my glass and watched it float between the ice cubes. "I'm really sorry you're going through this, Steph."

"Thanks. I guess that's why I came over. I needed the 'tea and sympathy.' "

I smiled and noticed another plumeria flower being tugged from the tree by invisible fingers that sent it into a free fall. The fragrant offering landed softly on the grass. Later that afternoon, I would collect the scattered beauties and string them together to make a unique gift, a homemade lei to welcome someone special who was arriving on the island at sunset.

"You're in a free fall, aren't you?" I suggested.

"Is that what it is? I was thinking it feels more like I'm a victim."

"A victim?"

"Yes. A victim of all the uncomfortable circumstances going on. I have no control over what's happening. Everyone else seems to be making the decisions about our future." She leaned back and gave a sigh. "I know God is in control. But I still feel like a victim."

We sat together in silence for a moment. I leaned closer. "May I tell you a story? A true story?"

Between here and heaven, every minute that the Christian lives will be a minute of grace.
—Charles Spurgeon

Steph knows me well, so my question made her grin. "It's what you do," she said. "Yes. Please. Tell me a story."

"Two days after our son's thirteenth birthday, I walked into a building in downtown Portland in broad daylight. I was taken into a back room where all my clothes were removed. A man wearing a mask knocked me out. While I was unconscious, another masked man thrust a knife into my abdomen. Twice."

Steph's jaw went slack.

"When I finally came to, I was in a hospital bed with dozens of sutures holding my midriff together. I had done nothing to deserve what happened to me."

"I never heard this before! I can't believe it. Why would anyone do that to you?"

I tried to keep my expression steady as I gave her the bigger picture of the traumatic experience. "The building I walked into was a hospital. Providence Medical Center, to be exact. The man who rendered me unconscious was an anesthesiologist."

"What?"

"The masked man with the knife was a surgeon. He removed several diseased masses and repaired my bile duct. I have a nine-inch scar right here." I traced a diagonal line across my torso. "And another six-inch scar here."

Steph narrowed her eyes. She looked like she might throw something at me. "Why didn't you just say you had your gallbladder removed?"

I laughed. "Because the experience sounds so different when you don't know the final outcome ahead of time. That's what you're going through right now; lots of painful steps without knowing the final punch line. When I only told you the painful facts of my experience, it seemed as though I were a victim of an act of violence."

"It certainly did. But, obviously, the big picture is that the surgery was for your good. You're still alive."

"Yes, I am." I drew my shoulders back and smiled. "I'm still here, twenty years later. So, I guess you could say that it's true: I was a victim. I was a victim of grace."

Steph put her glass of plantation tea on the end table. Our voices lowered as we talked about the mysterious ways of God, his timing, and the challenge of seeing more than just the circumstances in our life experiences. We reminded each other of times in our lives when God accomplished his purposes in us and through us even though we couldn't see the big picture and didn't understand the difficult things we were going through.

As Steph stood to leave, she said, "I wish more people would tell the uncomfortable parts of their story instead of just the punch line. We need to know we're not alone in the process, especially when it's painful."

We walked together to her car, gave each other a hug, and I returned to the backyard where I went about gathering plumerias, selecting just the right ones for the lei. I thought of how the lovely flowers had ended up on the grass after their free fall. All that beauty scattered at my feet, ready to be collected. Before me were dozens of delicate, uncomplaining victims of the unseen hand that had plucked them from the tree.

As I strung the flowers on the long lei needle, Steph's earlier comment about how we need to know we're not alone echoed in my thoughts. She had said she wished more people would tell the uncomfortable parts of their stories. We need to see the big picture and not just the punch line.

It occurred to me that that was what God did when he recorded the true tales of many of the women in the Bible. He didn't airbrush their lives or make excuses for their choices. He showed them as they were. Real. Human. Flawed. And also deeply loved by the One who fashioned them by hand and knew them by heart. Their stories are scattered throughout Scripture, ready to be gathered up. I wondered how many of them could see the big picture when they were in the midst of their own difficult experience.

The scent of afternoon rain breezed my way. I could smell the rain before I could see the misty drops. As I watched, the fluid grace gently covered, nourished, cleansed, and restored everything within view.

My thoughts ran to a deep place. I considered how there is nothing I can do, nothing to make the rain fall or the wind blow. Unprovoked by any act on my part, God gives me breath. He opens his hand and gives and gives and gives. I don't control his faithfulness. I don't initiate his mercy. I can do nothing to earn his kindness. I don't deserve his gifts.

The truth is, I am powerless to stop his love for me.

I did nothing to activate his goodness toward me. I am incapable of deflecting the endless showers of blessings that come from his storehouses and rain over my life. It's all grace. Grace upon grace. God's extravagant grace.

Indeed, I am a victim of grace.

And so are you.

Grace: (noun) a manifestation of unmerited favor

Returning to the fresh flowers cradled in my lap, I finished stringing the lei and tied the two ends together. I thought about how God gifted me to tell stories. In recent years I've been invited to speak around the world, and at each event, I'm asked to tell stories. I have stood before thousands and told true stories of how God manifests his unmerited favor in the lives of ordinary women.

Drawing in the fragrance of the lei in my hands, I wondered what it would look like if I gathered up my free-fall stories and strung them together side-by-side with stories of some of the women in the Bible. What if I shared, as one friend shares with another, the uncomfortable parts of the journey as well as the beauty of what happens when God's goodness prevails? I had a pretty good idea that the result would not be one long, meandering line, but rather, as each story touched the next, it would connect just right and turn into a full circle, like a lei.

In the same way that a lei is created so that it can be presented as a gift, I now offer this gift of full-circle stories to you, dear kindred victim of grace. May you see the big picture of your own story on these pages and may it be evident that God's goodness is prevailing even when you can't see the final punch line.

Chapter 2

THE DREAM THAT WOULD NOT GO AWAY

When I was twelve, a small dream took root inside of me. That dream grew and would not go away. I knew the dream was odd, especially for a preteen. But there it was, deeply embedded in my heart. I wanted to be a missionary.

From the moment I first saw a slide of a sunset at the end of a foreign-missions presentation, I knew that was what I wanted to do with my life. I wanted to travel around the world and tell people about God's love. I wanted to translate God's stories in a way that people who had never heard them would be drawn in and want to know him more.

I shared my dream with my counselor at summer camp, and she said, "You can start by being a missionary at home."

So, while I was in middle school, I started a Christian club in the cafeteria at lunchtime. In high school I persuaded friends to come to church with me, and I went on numerous missions trips to Mexico. My closest friends were missionary kids, and I secretly envied their childhoods spent in foreign lands among interesting cultures. My college roommate, Marjie, spoke fluent Spanish because she was a missionary kid from Colombia. I was certain she had experienced more adventure in her eighteen years in South America than I ever had growing up in Southern California and spending my summers at Newport Beach with friends from church.

I couldn't wait to leave my familiar, comfortable surroundings and do something significant for God out there in the bigger world.

But during my sophomore year in college, my heart took a detour. I fell in love. My boyfriend and I became engaged a few weeks after he graduated from the Christian college we both attended. I understood that our future would not be spent on the mission field. That wasn't his calling. But it was okay. We'd have a good life together. After all, we were in love.

Or so I thought.

On a cold February afternoon the following year, he looked me in the eye and said it wasn't going to work. He didn't love me. He said that one day I would thank him for making this decision for both of us.

My wedding dress was hanging in the closet. The invitations had been selected and were on hold at the printer. As I slid the engagement ring off my finger, the painful reality of what had just happened pounded in my ears. I was unwanted. Rejected.

During that season of my life, if the term *victim of grace* had flitted through my thoughts, it wouldn't have found a place to land. I hurt. Ached. All I knew was the blistering sting of rejection. I didn't dare think that God was accomplishing some ultimate good in my life through this.

I just wanted to be alone.

As an expression of true sisterhood, my friend Luanne came over to be with me on the night of my disengagement. She told me I needed a new dream. Then she did two smart things. First, she drove me to a restaurant, where she ordered hamburgers for both of us and coaxed me to take a few bites. Next, she asked if there was anything I wanted to do or any place I'd wanted to visit.

"I always wanted to go to Hawaii," I said. "Or Austria."

With a wave of her hand, Luanne made another decision for both of us. "I've been to Hawaii. You can go there another time. Let's go to Austria this summer. We can see if the hills really are alive with the sound of music. And we can go to Germany too. And Switzerland. And ..."

Her words of hope for the future released a wellspring of tears. She pushed the hamburger closer, but I couldn't eat until I told her about The Dream That Would Not Go Away—how it had been in my heart to go to the ends of the earth. I confessed that I had put it aside when my heart became all twitterpated over getting married. Wishes of seeing more of this wide world had been willingly relinquished in exchange for plans for a bridal shower, a studio apartment, and a shared car payment with someone who didn't want to travel the globe.

"Then let this new dream be part of The Dream That Would Not Go Away," Luanne told me. "You can stay on in Europe after our jaunt and find a missions organization that needs some short-term help."

She made it sound so easy. And it was.

Four months later, I boarded a plane for the first time in my life, and we were on our way across "the pond." The ministry opportunity presented itself naturally while I was in Europe. I served as a courier, a smuggler. I traveled behind the Iron Curtain with three other young women to deliver thousands of Bibles to believers in underground churches in the former Soviet Union.

When I returned to Southern California, I was a changed woman and certain that I was ready to become a full-time missionary. The next step was attending the Urbana Student Missions Conference, where I hoped to receive direction on where I would spend the rest of my life serving the Lord after I finished college.

At the conference, I filled out an important form, carefully and prayerfully checking the boxes next to the terms that best described my unique gifting, interests, and abilities. That form was fed into the grand computer (circa 1977) to match up my skills and calling with the right ministry opening in some remote corner of the world.

As I stood in line at the conference, sporting long, seventies-style hair and wearing an embroidered muslin shirt from Mexico, I couldn't wait to receive the printout with the answer. What challenging and amazing position on the mission field awaited someone with my unique gifts and skills?

When the printout finally emerged, I held my breath and read the words: *Laundry Supervisor, Nairobi, Kenya.*

Silence. Blink. Shuffle. Blink again.

Not exactly what I'd expected, but there it was. God's will for my life.

I applied for the position of laundry supervisor and waited for the confirmation letter.

Around that time, the movie *The Hiding Place* debuted in theaters. It told the real-life story of Corrie ten Boom, a prisoner in a Nazi concentration camp during World War II. I had taken a job as an assistant in the Southern California office where all the mail for Corrie was processed and met *Tante* (Aunt) Corrie, as those who worked there called her. I also read her books, including *Tramp for the Lord.*

I loved this Rosey Posey of a woman and longed to go to exotic places like Corrie did and tell people about God's great love for his children. It looked as if that exotic place for me was going to be Africa and not Eastern Europe, as I had thought it might be after my summer adventure as a Bible smuggler.

When I met with the teen girls in the Sunday school class I taught, I told them, "Pray for me, girls! I'm going to Africa."

"Why?" they asked.

"I'm going to be a laundry supervisor."

Blank stares. "What exactly will you do as a laundry supervisor?" they wanted to know.

I went a little overboard, I'm sure, as I spun the tale that had been forming in my imagination. "I'm going to learn how to carry a big basket on my head. Every day I'll walk down to the river and join the women of the village. We'll work together, side by side, singing, laughing, telling stories. The children will play beside us as we do the laundry. This is how I'm going to serve the Lord."

Each week the girls wanted to hear more about Africa, and I kept the stories coming, embellishing to my heart's content. Soon the girls were confiding that they hoped one day that they too would be selected to serve as laundry supervisors in Africa. They wanted to see the land where baby elephants bathed and laughing children splashed about in the river under the warm sun, and where women plunged the dirty laundry of Nairobi into the same river that flowed with the pure waters of Mount Kilimanjaro.

But I trust in you, Lord;
I say, "You are my God."
My times are in your hands.
—Psalm 31:14–15

At last, many months after the Urbana conference, the response from the mission in Kenya arrived. I tore open the envelope and read the letter. My heart sank.

They turned me down. I was rejected. Again.

The letter stated that my "specific skills" weren't a "sufficient match" for the position. All I took in was the message hidden between the lines: I was unwanted. A loser. No one wanted to marry me, and now I couldn't even wash clothes for Jesus in Africa.

A few days later, I stood before the girls in my Sunday school class, letter in hand. With a weighted spirit, I gave my sad report: "You can stop praying. I'm not going to Africa. I didn't get the position."

One of the girls unsympathetically popped off with, "Good. We don't want you to leave. We want you to stay here. We think you should find a job telling stories. We love it when you tell us stories."

Something deep and shame-filled inside me winced at her suggestion. My self-image curled up into a ball like a roly-poly bug. I didn't want to be a writer. I didn't like that telling stories had always been easy for me.

Growing up, I got in trouble for telling stories. Teachers called it "lying." My sister called it "exaggerating—again." My parents would do the twirling-finger sign at the dinner table, indicating that I should speed up my monologue and get to the point.

No. I did not want to be a writer. Telling stories got me in trouble. I didn't see my imaginative way of thinking as a gift.

It wasn't that I was trying to be dishonest when I told stories. I was only repeating what I saw in my imagination. And I only shared a small portion of what I saw. I learned early on to keep the rest of the whimsy to myself. No one wanted to hear about the images that chummed around in my mind—images of a kangaroo eating Cheerios out of the palm of my hand, of me singing at the top of my lungs from the Eiffel Tower, or of spending a warm winter night sleeping under the stars in a hammock strung between two palm trees.

All fanciful notions needed to be snuffed out, including The Dream That Would Not Go Away. I wasn't special. I wasn't missionary material. I needed to be more like everyone else and live a normal life.

So instead of returning to finish college, I found a respectable job at a bank where I used colorless, unbending numbers every day instead of vibrant, lithe, storytelling words. And I fell in love again. This time to a man who loved God and loved me—and who knew who he was.

This new dream, I found, wasn't a bad dream at all: loving and being loved, marrying a godly man, putting my whole heart into making a cozy home, giving birth to two wonderful children and raising them together, serving alongside my husband in youth ministry. We had a good life.

My insightful husband urged me to develop my natural storytelling ability and sent me to a writers' conference. I learned how to write devotions and articles and, to my surprise, the first few articles I submitted were accepted for publication. Accepted is such a wonderful word! I started working on a series of books for toddlers and knew deep down I should be grateful for all that God had done. And I was.

But somehow I couldn't shake the quiet sadness that came over me whenever I heard an inspiring story of someone who served overseas and was working among an unreached people group. That had been my dream. And here I was, almost thirty, still living in California, changing diapers and writing children's books. If this was how God was fulfilling his purpose for me, then why did he plant such crazy dreams in my heart so long ago? Where were the elephants?

I put aside all hopes of traveling to unknown corners of the world and for the next ten years I lived the life that had been given to me. During that time I kept writing, I kept loving my husband and our children, and I was grateful. Very grateful. It was not difficult to convince myself that it was enough. Life was abundant.

A Kindred Victim of Grace

Then came the surgery that altered my forty-year-old body as well as my overall health and mental outlook.

A nagging pain in my side followed by abnormal lab results sent me into the hospital. My husband and I thought I'd only be there overnight, not for a week. The "masked man with the knife" determined that it was necessary to remove more than just my gallbladder. A separate incision was made to extract two enlarged cysts, repair my colon, and remove my appendix. I was sent home to heal and instead of inviting Faith and Hope to be my companions during the convalescence, I allowed Fear to make himself comfortable on the end of my bed where he peppered me with vile questions:

What if more rogue cells still are inside you? What if they are multiplying at this very moment, just waiting to take you down?

What will happen to your husband and children if you die?

What about all your unfinished projects and unfulfilled dreams?

When Fear paused long enough to catch his breath, Doubt was right there beside him, ready to carry on the bedside vigil. The two of them delighted in taking turns at telling me how my life would end and convincing me it had been a small life, really. The Dream That Would Not Go Away would become the Dream That Never Was.

The worst part was that I listened to them. I could have told them to go away, to be gone, in the name of Jesus. But I didn't. I didn't speak the golden command that would make them flee. I didn't choose to believe that God was accomplishing his purpose for me and that my times were in his hands. After many days of feeling overwhelmed with pain and deep discouragement, I finally turned to God's Word. In the book of 1 Samuel I found the story of a kindred victim of grace. Her name was Hannah. For years she had longed for a baby, but she couldn't conceive. Fear and Doubt must have assigned themselves to be her travel companions, plaguing her with their life-sapping accusations as she and her husband made their yearly pilgrimage to Shiloh. The effects of those two unwelcome companions and their accusations have played out the same way from generation to generation.

By the time Hannah arrived at the feast, she was heartbroken and wept a thousand tears. I knew exactly how she felt.

Her husband said, "Why be downhearted just because you have no children? You have me—isn't that better than having ten sons?" (1:8 NLT).

No! My spirit answered loud and clear for Hannah. We were sisters at heart across many centuries, and I knew her answer had to be, *It is not better! It is not the same as having a Dream That Would Not Go Away.* Hannah's dream was to have a child. Mine was to be a missionary. Neither of us had been successful in fulfilling our own dreams and the older we got the more impossible it seemed.

Hannah left the feast. She went to find a private place in the temple where she could pray. In her deep anguish she wept bitterly, crying out to the Lord. Hannah pleaded with God to give her a son. Just one child. That's all she asked. Just one. She made a vow, promising the LORD Almighty, or literally, "the Lord of Heaven's Armies," that if he gave her a son, she would dedicate him to be a servant in the Lord's temple as soon as he was old enough.

Eli the priest was sitting by the temple door watching Hannah as she prayed her heart out. It was a curious sight to him. As she prayed, her lips moved, but no sounds came out of her mouth.

How intensely focused her heart must have been on those prayers. How passionate and intimate were her expressions. She thought she was alone in the Lord's presence, and in her honesty before God, she gave the appearance of having lost control of her senses.

Eli concluded that she must be drunk. He toddled over to Hannah and told her to put away her wine and sober up.

The story doesn't reveal whether she told Eli the subject of her desperate prayers. Neither the specific problem nor her sincere vow were included in her response to him. She made no excuses for her actions or the way she appeared to Eli. It was enough for her to tell Eli these words:

"I'm a woman who is deeply troubled. I haven't been drinking wine or beer. I was telling the LORD all of my troubles. Don't think of me as an evil woman. I've been praying here because I'm very sad. My pain is so great" (verses 15–16 NIrV).

Eli then fulfilled his priestly role. He blessed her and said, "Go in peace, and may the God of Israel grant you what you have asked of him" (verse 17).

I wonder if either of them had any glimpse of the big picture at that point. That if God answered Hannah's prayer and gave her a son, and if she kept her vow and the child returned to serve in the temple, Eli would be the one who raised him. Regardless of what either of them understood at the moment, Eli's blessing must have filled Hannah with hope, because "she went her way and ate something, and her face was no longer downcast" (verse 18). Some things don't change in a thousand generations. Just as my friend Luanne had urged me to eat a little something, to be blessed, and to dream a new dream on the eve of my disengagement, Eli did the same for Hannah. The result was that Hannah went on her way with hope. Fear and Doubt had no choice but to spread their dark wings and fly away.

As I read about Hannah, I wanted to experience that same transformation; that same infusion of Hope. What would happen if I dared to dream again? What would those dreams look like in this season of life? They would certainly be different than the childhood dreams I'd clung to all these years.

Sequestered in the bedroom, confined to my bed, I followed Hannah's lead and poured out my heart to the Lord. I called upon the Lord Almighty, the Lord of Heaven's Armies, and when I did, Fear and Doubt fled. Hope returned. I tearfully asked the Lord to heal my body and restore my health. With soul-level honesty I relinquished my childhood dream and humbly asked, "So what is it that you want of me, Lord? What's next?"

Victim: (noun) from the Latin, *victima*, a live sacrifice

A line from a verse in Romans 12:1 settled in my thoughts. My Bible was still in my lap, so I turned there and found the verse: "Therefore, I urge you, brothers and sisters, in view of God's mercy, to offer your bodies as a living sacrifice, holy and pleasing to God—this is your true and proper worship."

The term *living sacrifice* stood out. This was the starting point if I was going to dare to dream a new dream. I needed to offer my body as a living sacrifice. His Word said that to do so was an act of worship and was pleasing to Him.

How can that be pleasing to you, Lord? You know how broken I am right now. I don't even have all my original parts. I'm so inadequate in so many ways.

I thought of Hannah, crying out to the Lord from a body that had been unable to conceive and carry new life. In spite of her inadequacies and her deep pain, she was willing to offer to God both her body and the life of her yet unborn son. Two living sacrifices.

Almighty God was asking the same of me; to willingly become a live sacrifice. And in doing so, I was becoming a victim. I was putting myself completely at the mercy of God. I surrendered anew, offering not only my body, but all that I was or ever would be. With deep longing, I asked God to give me a new dream, and then I asked him to give me Faith to fill up the space that Doubt had vacated in my spirit. Like Hannah, I immediately felt lifted. My countenance was no longer downcast.

I turned back to the book of 1 Samuel to find out what happened to Hannah. How did her story end? How did God answer her prayer?

The words are recorded with understated simplicity. The Lord remembered Hannah, and in the course of time, she became pregnant and gave birth to a son. Her dream came true. God's plan was fulfilled. Hannah named her son Samuel. And as she had promised, she consecrated Samuel to the Lord. When Samuel was old enough, she took him to Eli so that the boy might be trained to serve the Lord.

Hannah wrote a poem about her answered prayer, and God included it in his Book. That small slice of common ground between Hannah and me made me smile. Hannah was a writer. She wrote a poem and God published it. How could she ever have imagined that her poem would stay in print and be read 4,000 years later by another woman who was desperately in need of hope?

The LORD is good to all;
he has compassion on
all he has made.
—Psalm 145:9

I was about to close my Bible and give in to the nap my aching body was calling for when my gaze fell on one more verse in chapter 2 of 1 Samuel. There it was. An added whisper of hope.

"The LORD was gracious to Hannah … Over a period of years she had three more sons and two daughters" (verse 21 NIrV).

My heart began to pound wildly as I read the verse again and took in the abundance of those words. God gave Hannah six babies. Six!

And she had only asked him for one.

This is the extravagance of God. This is how he chose to bless a woman who surrendered everything to him. With Hannah's life example in mind, I dared to believe that I wasn't a victim of circumstances or genetic maladies. I was a living sacrifice and that made me a victim of grace; God's extravagant grace.

Chapter 3

EVERYTHING IS REDEEMABLE

"I know the plans I have for you," declares the LORD, *"plans to prosper you and not to harm you, plans to give you hope and a future."*

—JEREMIAH 29:11

Seven months after I read about Hannah from the confines of my bed, I was up and about, and our family started looking for a new place to live. During our house hunting, our nine-year-old daughter kept asking if we could buy a house with a gazebo in the front yard. She wanted to see the gazebo from her bedroom window.

My husband and I refrained from rolling our eyes and responded with the parental answer, "We'll see." We soon added "probably not" to the response.

Her descriptions grew to fairy-tale proportions when she talked about her dream of dancing in the gazebo, and how one day she was going to get married in a gazebo. We finally had to give her the cold, hard facts: "Honey, we're not going to move into a house with a gazebo."

"Where are we going to live?"

"We don't know yet. We haven't found a house. But we know it won't have a gazebo."

Undaunted, she asked her daddy, who could do anything, "Whatever house we move into, would you build me a gazebo? In the front yard, please."

His answer was the same all twenty-three times she asked. "No."

That was that.

We sorted and packed in preparation for the move—our seventh in six years. After so much shuffling and downsizing, I thought I'd gone through every box at least once before. Not so. This time I came across a manila envelope stuffed with old report cards. What I read gave me pause. My first-grade teacher had written on the back of my report card, "Robin has not yet grasped her basic math skills, but she does keep the entire class entertained at rug time."

There it was. Evidence that our daughter came by her fanciful wishes and imagination genetically. From my earliest years, I couldn't keep my imagination quiet, nor could I keep the expressions of my thoughts from coming out in story form.

Where do these foundational inklings inside us come from? Does God plant the seeds of our dreams deep within before we're born? Is it his bidding and his doing when those seeds take root and grow? How is it that some dreams seem to have been planted in us from the beginning and yet never grow tall, spread their frilly leaves, or bear luscious fruit? We all have whims and wishes that never came true. And yet we keep wishing. Why?

I thought about our daughter and how her father had given her a clear no about building a gazebo. My heavenly Father had given me a clear no on many things in my life. Good things as well as things that would not have been good for me. The things we hope for in life can't be wished into existence no matter how delightful or spiritual those possibilities might be. Why is that?

It seems to have very little to do with the dreams themselves but everything to do with the One who first planted the dreams inside us. God has been a Planter, a Gardener, from the beginning. He planted a garden east of Eden. He is the one who plants and uproots. God gives; God takes away.

As I was waiting to see what new dream might be springing up in my heart, I thought a lot about my long-term relationship with the Lord. The conclusion I came to was this: God is God. He can do whatever he wants. But what he wants most is a relationship with us.

Until we come to peace with the realization that a relationship with almighty God can happen only on his terms, not ours, we won't have an authentic relationship with him. As that truth permeated my heart, I realized that any dreams sprouting up in me were dreams that God was nurturing. If wishes lingered in my heart but weren't bearing fruit, most likely God was the one hindering their growth. The question was, what was bearing fruit in my life?

I am the Lord,
and there is no other.
I form the light and
create darkness.
I bring prosperity
and create disaster;
I, the Lord,
do all these things.
—Isaiah 45:6–7

The answer was right in front of me on the bookshelf. The new dream that had sprouted in my heart had nothing to do with Africa or laundry. This new dream was about telling stories. Then telling more stories. And then a few more.

Ironically, I had been working with several publishers for years by this time. More than thirty books had been published, and yet I still viewed storytelling as my downfall, my weakness. My natural bent toward embellishing was something I'd tried to hide. How could that impulse be a good thing?

From the moment a life is surrendered to Christ, the redeeming work of sanctification begins. My inclination to tell stories was being sifted in this sanctification process. My heart was being tested, my motives purified. Why would God carry out such a process in the life of a weak human?

A Kindred Victim of Grace

I found the answer in the life of another kindred victim of grace. Her name was Eve. She was the only woman not born into the wreckage all of us have shuffled through ever since the fall. Life for her on planet Earth was as God intended it to be.

Then one conversation changed everything. Words from the Deceiver led her to disobey God, even though she knew the penalty was death. And death did come. Spiritual death—that previously unexperienced place of being separated from God. Ongoing communion with God was lost.

As soon as Eve and Adam ate of the fruit, their eyes were opened. They looked at each other and saw their differences, their failings, their flaws. Their inadequacies were obvious.

That's when another death took place: the death of the first animal. The consequences of Adam and Eve's disobedience affected even the animals. God slayed an animal and used its skin to fashion coverings for Eve and her husband.

Love covers over a multitude of sins.

—1 Peter 4:8

Could it be that part of what was lost in the fall was a covering of grace? People who love each other know what that covering of grace looks like. They choose to love in spite of differences. They overlook flaws. They choose to extend grace—over and over and over. But when that love is removed and that covering of grace is taken away, certain death occurs in the relationship.

Adam and Eve knew what it was like to be in a relationship in which, despite all their quirks and differences, they weren't ashamed.

Not ashamed of their individual peculiarities, not ashamed of the other person's uniqueness and not ashamed of their flesh. But when their eyes were opened, they saw themselves and each other without that magnificent covering of grace. No longer able to look at each other through the eyes of unconditional love, they became painfully aware of their differences. Their disobedience led to death, and death had stripped them bare. For the first time since they were placed in the garden, they felt ashamed.

The solution seemed to be stitching together fig leaves as a man-made covering to hide their outward differences. Fig leaves, however, were inadequate. Only the invisible covering of perfect love and grace was sufficient for them. But now that covering was gone.

Fig leaves could never replace the covering God had provided. When the leaves were connected to the tree, they were living, green, and vibrant. When they were separated from that source of life, they slowly shriveled up and turned to dust. In Adam and Eve's separation from almighty God, their bodies would experience the same process of slowly shriveling and returning to dust.

Aware of what had happened, terrified and ashamed, Adam and Eve went into hiding.

So much pain. So much sorrow. Such a great loss.

Yet something happened on that day of catastrophic loss that draws in the rest of us with a gasp of hope. Yes, the paradise that Adam and Eve had known was lost through disobedience. The magnificent covering of unbridled love and grace was stripped away. Fellowship with the Creator was broken. A death sentence hung over their heads.

But in the midst of it all, God came. He made himself accessible.

While Adam and Eve were in hiding, they "heard the sound of the LORD God as he was walking in the garden in the cool of the day" (Genesis 3:8). They were awaiting their annihilation, and yet no lightning bolt struck them from the heavens. No invisible hand reached down and choked their last breath from them. Instead, the Lord God came to them in a very personal way. He came looking for them, seeking to restore what had been demolished. Even though they didn't ask for it, God was about to cover them with his love.

Adam and Eve were about to become the first victims of grace.

What did it sound like when the Lord God came walking in the garden? Were his footsteps heavy and earth pounding? Or was the sound of the Lord God more like a telling breeze or a rushing wind that set the birds to singing and the leaves of the trees to clapping their hands? Did he come with a gentle rain to wash away all that was soiled?

Whatever God sounded like when he walked in the garden in the cool of the day, Eve knew the sound. She knew it was God, not a deer or a rabbit or any other created being. It was God and God alone. And he was coming for her.

God called out, "Where are you?" (verse 9).

Eve was the first woman to hear the cry of the Relentless Lover. From that ancient moment until this very day, Father God hasn't stopped calling out to each of us. He comes walking in the garden of our hearts, pursuing us, making himself accessible, and inviting us to come out of hiding.

Why does he continue to do this millennia after millennia, when all of us continue to disobey? We go into hiding, inadequately covered from the fear and shame that paralyze us. Yet God, the Relentless Lover, comes walking in the gardens of our hearts, calling out, "Where are you?" because we are his first love, and he wants us back.

Certainly God knew right where Adam and Eve were when he called out his passionate question. No one and nothing is hidden from him.

Could it be that his question was an invitation? By answering him, Adam and Eve were responding to God's gesture of mercy. He didn't demolish them as they had demolished their relationship with him. God didn't wipe them off the face of the earth. He didn't ignore them and leave them in their terror and misery.

He came to them. He invited them to respond to his question. In this first expression of an extraordinary and extravagant outpouring of grace, God established through their lives the theme of his Book: everything is redeemable.

Do we still believe that today? Every life can be ransomed. That which was broken and worthless can be restored. Everything is redeemable.

What happens when we come out of hiding, are honest with God, and receive the provisions he has prepared for us?

For Eve it meant that she lived. Her days on earth were extended. God provided the skin of an animal to cover her nakedness. Eve was the first woman to give birth, the first mother to experience the joy of cradling her child and kissing his brow as he slept in her arms.

A bittersweet mercy.

We know this same mercy because we also deserve death. But just like Eve, we got "graced." God has provided a way for us to return to communion with him. In spite of all our failings, he remains faithful. Always. Forever. He continues to beckon us into a closer relationship with him. Everything in our lives is still redeemable. Hope pervades every situation because grace covers us like the handmade clothing God gave Eve. A covering that was provided only by the shedding of blood.

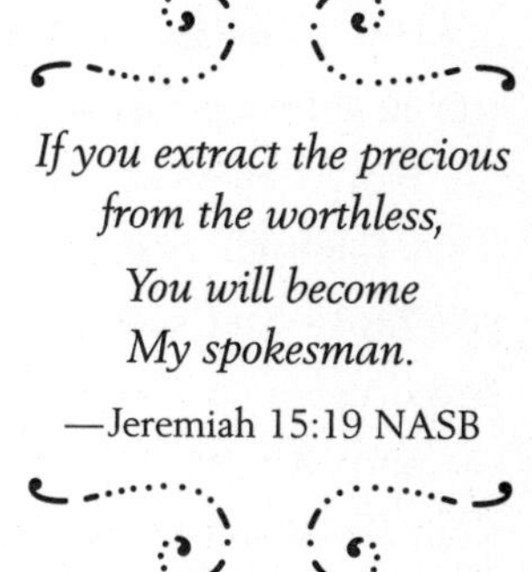

If you extract the precious
from the worthless,
You will become
My spokesman.
—Jeremiah 15:19 NASB

As I looked back over my life, I saw evidence of this sanctification at work as my childhood propensity toward exaggeration and "lying" was redeemed and transformed into the craft of storytelling. The Lord turned what I saw as a weakness I was ashamed of into a strength that was accomplishing his purposes. I wonder what would have happened to that "bent" in my personality if God hadn't redeemed it.

Retracing the Steps to Discover the Treasure

I thought back to those girls in my Sunday school class who said they were glad I wasn't going to Africa to wash clothes, because they wanted me to keep telling stories. At the time, their suggestion seemed like a bad idea. I saw my inclination toward telling tales as a bad habit that needed to be purged from my life.

Even so, I began to wonder whether my tendency toward telling tales could be used for good instead of getting me into trouble.

My husband believed it could. He urged me to attend a writers' conference soon after we were married. One of the speakers delivered a memorable talk on what Paul must have meant when he told Timothy to "stir up the gift of God which is in you" (2 Timothy 1:6 NKJV).

I knew I had words in me, and that those words needed to find a way to line up and dance into the world in some useful way. If this was how God created me, then certainly he had a purpose for me, a specific use for this gift of storytelling. I felt like I needed to be a good steward of the gift, but I didn't fully see my ability as a treasure.

During the first five years of our marriage, I struggled with my work at the bank, making numbers, not words, line up and march across the page with precision. The process drained me, discouraged me. But I needed a job, and this was the one that met our needs. That's why I stayed there for half a decade.

However, nearly every day at noon, I would take my sack lunch and leave the main branch of Oceanside Federal Savings and Loan. I'd walk two blocks to the small Christian bookstore next to the ice-cream shop and do some market research. Danielle and her staff always welcomed me and let me eat my lunch in the beanbag chair in the children's section. If it wasn't busy, they'd let me interview them and take notes in my journal.

"What sorts of books do people come in asking for that you don't have?"

"What books are the most popular?"

"Who is your favorite author? Why?"

On many afternoons I sat in the children's section nibbling my sandwich and writing anything and everything that came to mind. I had no idea how to be a writer, but after attending the weekend writers' conference at Forest Home, I did have an idea of where to start. I needed to get an article published. Then I could honestly say I was a published author.

I wrote and rewrote a short devotional piece for *The Upper Room* about a Christian I had met while smuggling Bibles into what was then Czechoslovakia. I also shared that nothing in life is wasted. Everything is redeemable. Even experiences on a summer missions trip.

It was a banner day when my acceptance letter finally arrived in the mail. The magazine offered to pay me ten dollars for 612 words. All I had to do was fill out the form stating my name as it should appear in print. I printed my married name on the form and left it on the kitchen counter.

My parents came by that evening for a visit, and I told them the good news that I was about to become a published author. My dad took one look at the form and scowled. "That's not right," he mumbled.

"What's not right?"

"Your name. You've been a Jones a lot longer than you've been a Gunn. Give our side of the family some credit here."

I immediately crossed out Robin Gunn and penned what would become my official signature: Robin Jones Gunn. I looked at my dad for his approval, and my heart soared when he gave me one of his wonderful winks. This was our insiders' secret. I was Robin Jones Gunn, and my father, the son of a Kentucky coal miner, was proud of me.

After that first devotional was published, it became a fun hobby to see where else I might submit an article, poem, or short story. I took a creative writing course at the community college and signed up for the Write to Publish program.

When our first child was born, I read children's books to him. But before he was a year old, I had written my own series of six toddlers' books titled Billy 'n' Bear.

The first few publishers I contacted turned down the series. That was okay. My son liked the stories, and that was why I'd written them. I was content to use the books for that purpose alone.

Another young mom, Jacque, kept suggesting publishing houses that might be interested in the stories, so I pursued those leads as well. In the meantime, I continued to write articles and find as many ways as possible to make money at home so I wouldn't have to return to the bank job after maternity leave. I typed résumés, took in other babies for day care, sold cosmetics at home parties, and handed out food samples at grocery stores.

All the side jobs came and went, but my drive to write continued to grow. More than anything it was an act of obedience. The income was essential to supplement my husband's youth pastor salary.

By the time the Billy 'n' Bear Series was accepted by Concordia Publishing House, I had almost fifty articles and interviews in print. Two more series of books for toddlers were soon published, and yet I didn't consider myself to be a "real" writer. I much preferred to stay in the background, working beside my husband with the youth group or hanging out in the church nursery with our son.

Covering up my small successes and going into hiding felt like a safe thing to do. I grew nervous when people asked me about being published, because I didn't really know what I was doing. I still thought I'd missed the mark. After all, I hadn't become a missionary. My earthly father might be proud of me, but inside I wondered if my heavenly Father had any reason to give me a wink of approval. Was God pleased with me?

I didn't yet understand that fretting about being good enough in God's eyes was a result of living under the law and being focused on works. My redeemed life in Christ could only be experienced to the fullest by living in the unforced rhythms of his grace.

The motivation and the focus of my writing efforts took an unexpected turn while we were on a camping trip with seventy teenagers at San Clemente State Beach. I found several of the girls hiding in their tent one sunny day. I got on my knees, crawled into the tent, and said, "What are you girls doing in here? There's sun, surf, sand, and boys out there. Why are you hiding out in here?"

"We're reading," they replied.

"What are you reading?" I saw the stack of two-dozen novels they had brought with them from the library. Their idea of a fun time was reading about adventures rather than going outside and actually having an adventure of their own.

He saved us, not because of righteous things we had done, but because of his mercy.

—Titus 3:5

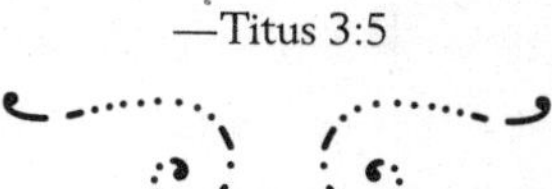

"Mind if I read with you?" I said.

They handed me three of their favorite books. The first book made me bite my lip as I read. The second caused me to clench my teeth. By the third book I couldn't read anymore.

"That's it," I told them. "I don't want you reading these books. They are way too evocative. You're thirteen years old! Do your mothers know this is what you're reading? I don't want you putting these stories in your young hearts. Everything I've just read is the opposite of what I've been teaching you each week in Sunday school. Read something else."

"Like what?" they asked.

"I don't know. I'll find some different books for you. But for now, how about if you go down to the beach and start a new chapter in your own life stories?"

After the camping trip, the search for appropriate teenage fiction began. I found a few novels at the Christian bookstore and delivered them to the girls at church on Sunday. By Wednesday-night youth group, they returned the books, saying they had read them all and wanted more.

"There aren't any more," I told them. "Can't you read those ones again?"

"We've already read them twice."

Then one of the girls came up with a brilliant idea. "Why don't you write some books for us?"

"Oh no, I could never do that," I insisted.

"But you've already written a bunch of books," she said.

"Those books are for toddlers. They only have eight words on each page. I could never write a whole novel."

The girls looked at each other and then turned to me with a sense of finality. "Yes, you can," they said. "We'll help you. We'll tell you what to write. How hard could that be?"

It turned out to be very hard. Writing a novel for a group of discerning teens is a humbling experience. Every week I would take a chapter with me to Sunday school. After I had taught the lesson, I would use the last fifteen minutes of class to read the chapter to the girls. They were honest critics and never hesitated to speak their minds. They told me everything I did wrong and everything I needed to change, including the characters' names.

I wrote about Uncle Bob and Aunt Bonnie; they changed the names to Uncle Bob and Aunt Marti. I wrote about Ron and Christy. They changed the names to Todd and Christy.

Each week the girls expected a new chapter or a revised version of the chapter they'd rejected the week before. That meant I had to write fast, which was difficult to do in the midst of our busy ministry and caring for a toddler.

During that time I happened upon a paperback by C. S. Lewis that I had bought for a class in college. *Letters to an American Lady* was a collection of letters Lewis wrote to—you guessed it—an American lady, whose name was Mary. The two of them carried on a correspondence from 1950 until Lewis's death in 1963.

At the end of a letter written on September 30, 1958, Jack, as he was called by his friends, wrote, "I'm a barbarously early riser and have usually got my breakfast and dealt with my letters before the rest of the house is astir. One result is that I often enjoy the only fine hours of the day.... I love the empty, silent, dewy, cobwebby hours."[1]

I tried to picture Lewis in the Kilns, the house where he lived in Oxford that was described as "a house of books held together by cobwebs."[2]

I wondered what sort of proper teapot Jack used, and whether he took his tea with milk and sugar when he prepared his breakfast before "the rest of the house [was] astir." What did he see out the window of his cottage in those "cobwebby hours" of the morning?

I was certain I would never know. It was too impossible a dream that I might go to England one day and see his home.

I settled for trying out Lewis's work ethic. To make the whole experiment jolly, I went right out and bought myself a proper teapot and a box of English breakfast tea. I set my alarm for 3:00 a.m. and got up to write pages and pages about Todd and Christy while my household was still sleeping. The plan worked.

The phone never rang, my thoughts were always fresh, and I became a bit of a tea lover. That set-aside portion of the day, from 3:00 a.m. to 7:00 a.m., three days each week, continued to be my regular writing time for decades.

During the two years I was working on the first Christy Miller novel, I sent off what I had completed to ten publishers. All ten turned it down. Rejected once again! I was familiar with rejection. Unlike the rejection from my broken engagement or the missions letter from Kenya that said I lacked the required skills for the laundry-supervisor position, the most common response from publishers was that there was no market for a teen novel. They didn't know where they would find readers for such a book.

---

1 C. S. Lewis, *Letters to an American Lady* (Grand Rapids: Eerdmans, 1967), 78.

2 Evelyn Tan Powers, "U.S. Group Fixes C. S. Lewis House," *USA Today*, August 23–25, 1996, http://www.cslewis.org/about/press/1996usatoday.html.

I wanted to reply to each publisher (but never did), "Do you want to know where you can find the readers? They're hiding! In camping tents, in their bedrooms, on porch swings. Go see what your daughter is reading right now. Find out what books are coming home with her from school. What library books has she checked out? That's where you'll find the market."

When I was pregnant with our second child, life was difficult on many levels. Rewriting again and again was neither fun nor easy, and I found the weekly criticism of my teenage critics and the consistent rejections from publishers demoralizing. Our finances were at an all-time low. I was ready to give up on ever getting that first Christy Miller book published.

But what kept me going were the girls in my Sunday school class and a Bible verse I came across that changed the way I viewed this exercise in defeat. I wrote the verse on a card, which I framed and placed on the kitchen windowsill so I would see it whenever I washed dishes. On the card was a Victorian painting of a mother cuddled up with her young daughter reading a book together. The verse I wrote on the card was Psalm 102:18: "Let this be written for a future generation, that a people not yet created may praise the LORD."

I didn't know if the child I carried was a boy or a girl, but I did know that he or she would be part of a future generation. What sorts of stories would my children have to read?

I decided that when I finished the Christy Miller book, I would make my own copies if no one wanted to publish it. This was before the days of inexpensive self-publishing or any sort of e-publishing. Even using a photocopy machine to print copies that I could place in a binder was an expense far beyond my budget. So I planned to mimeograph enough copies for the girls in my Sunday school class, with an extra copy for me in case I had a daughter. Maybe she would want to read this story someday.

When the book was finally finished, I hosted a breakfast party at our house for all the girls in my Sunday school class. Raising their glasses of orange juice in a toast, they told me they approved of how the story turned out. It was as much their story as it was mine, and together we celebrated the victory of completing the work. It had taken two years, and now these girls were fifteen. Can you guess what those fifteen-year-olds told me? They said they wanted more books. More stories.

"We need more role models like Christy and Todd and the rest of the gang. You tell us things about God when you teach, but when you write about them in a story, we remember them. Your stories change us on the inside."

If their assessment was true, I knew the heart-change piece had to be something God did in and through the characters. I certainly didn't know how to accomplish something eternal like that.

Undaunted by the lack of interest from publishers in my first teenage novel, I bought a ream of paper and asked permission to use the church's mimeograph machine. The girls in my class pressed me to provide them with copies of the book they had helped me write.

Then, on a Monday afternoon in January 1988, everything changed.

I was standing in the driveway as our five-year-old son rode his tricycle up to the tree at the neighbor's house and then back to the cracked sidewalk line at the end of our driveway. Our second child had been born eight months earlier. A daughter! A wish come true. She clung to me in the driveway, watching her brother do spins on his tricycle and then pedal like a whirlwind down to the neighbor's tree and back.

Our new cordless phone was as large as a man's shoe. I'd placed it on the front step, anticipating a call from my husband saying what time he was coming home for lunch. When the phone rang, I reached for it, balanced the chunk of "modern" technology on my shoulder, and tried to keep my daughter from pulling it away.

The caller wasn't my husband. It was an editor. A real, true, big-time editor at a publishing house. She spoke the words that altered my life.

"We would like to publish your book."

After two years of rising at 3:00 a.m. three days a week, ten rejections, dozens of rewrites, and hundreds of cups of tea, *Summer Promise*, the first Christy Miller story, was going to be published by Focus on the Family. The baby daughter in my arms, who hadn't even yet been wished for when I started writing this book for teens, would now have a copy of a real book to read one day.

A few weeks after *Summer Promise* was released, a letter from a teen arrived at the publishing house. She said she had read the book and had made a life-changing decision. When she read the part where Christy prayed to surrender her life to Christ, the teen realized that she had never given her life to Christ. Just like Christy, she thought she was a Christian because she went to church with her parents. Her response was to pray right along with Christy and commit her life to the Lord.

The letter made me weep. This one letter made all the hours, rewrites, and rejections worth it. I held in my hand evidence that everything is redeemable. But that wasn't the end of it. Letters from teen girls continued to come with one salvation story after another. Dozens—and then hundreds—of readers were surrendering their lives to Christ after reading the first Christy Miller book.

The writing journey had befuddled, humbled, and amazed me in ways I had never experienced before. I felt like Eric Liddell in the film *Chariots of Fire* when he said, "[God] made me fast. And when I run I feel his pleasure."[3]

God made me a storyteller, and when I wrote, I felt his pleasure.

Right after the publication of the first Christy Miller book, the publisher asked for a sequel. And then another. And another.

We tucked away enough money over the years until we were finally able to buy our own home. It seemed like a dream we never thought would come true.

3 *Chariots of Fire*, directed by Hugh Hudson, Twentieth Century Fox, 1981.

The Realtor took us to see a house near Portland that was part of a new housing development. The abiding wish of our romantic nine-year-old daughter hadn't wavered. She still wanted a gazebo. We pulled up and all of us could see that this house had a lovely cedar tree in the front yard, but no gazebo.

Our Realtor led us upstairs, showed our daughter the room that might be hers, and asked, "Do you see that muddy field?"

Of course we saw it. That was all we could see across the street from that bedroom window.

The Realtor continued, "That whole area is going to be a park with grass and ..."

"A playground?" our son interrupted, looking hopeful.

"No, not a playground," she said. "But it will have a gazebo. Right there." She gestured toward the field.

We looked at each other, stunned.

"A gazebo?" I squeaked. "In clear view of our daughter's bedroom window? Are you sure?"

"Yes. Why? Did I say something wrong?" the Realtor asked.

"No, you said something right," my husband said.

Without a hint of surprise, our daughter smiled. Her blue eyes sparkled. "I knew there would be a gazebo. My daddy said no, so I asked God for one."

How did God do that? I wanted to know. Did he plant the winsome dream in our daughter's heart? Or did the wish grow in her imagination because her heavenly Father wanted to grace her with this very specific gift in order to reveal himself to her young heart?

Either way, it was clear that God was giving all of us evidence that he does have plans for us that are good plans. He delights in giving us a future and a hope.

I saw that truth revealed again on a stormy Northwest afternoon, five years after we moved into the new house. I paused as I walked past our daughter's bedroom. Outside her window, raindrops glistened as they dripped from the gingerbread trim along the top of the gazebo in the park across the street. She was stretched out on her bed reading the Christy Miller series as if those stories had been written just for her.

My heart skipped a beat as I remembered the verse in Psalm 102:18 that I'd written on a card almost fifteen years earlier, before I knew if the child I carried was a boy or a girl. I hadn't forgotten how fervently I'd prayed that the book my daughter was now reading would be, as the verse said, "written for a future generation, that a people not yet created may praise the LORD." That prayer was being answered right before my eyes.

As I turned to go, she called me into her room.

"Mom, do you think God has a guy like Todd for me out there?" she asked.

My first thought was to use the familiar parental answer of "we'll see," but that had never worked with her, and I was sure it wouldn't work now. Yet I didn't want to promise her something I couldn't guarantee.

"I know that God has plans for you," I said. "And his plans for you are for good, not for evil, to bring you a future and a hope. That's what God promises in his Word."

My daughter put her nose back in her book and, without looking at me, said, "I'm glad you wrote this book, Mom. It makes me want to love God more. And if he does have a Todd out there for me, I want to save myself for him."

What mother, from Eve until now, could wish for more than that for her child?

Chapter 4

A BLESSING INSIDE THE OBEDIENCE

You know with all your heart and soul that not one of all the good promises the LORD your God gave you has failed. Every promise has been fulfilled; not one has failed.

—JOSHUA 23:14

During the eight years it took me to write all twelve of the Christy Miller books, our family had moved a lot. In one particularly difficult season, we spent five months living at my parents' home. The four of us shared a single downstairs bedroom along with the washer and dryer. After that we relocated in Reno, Nevada, where we worked with college students for three years. The next move took us to Portland, Oregon, where we rented a one-hundred-year-old house that had one bathroom with its original claw-foot bathtub. The house was only a few blocks from the seminary my husband attended while working on a master's in counseling. Every place we lived was clearly God's provision for us in that season. But since we were always renting it never quite felt as if we were "home."

Around the time we moved to Portland, I was asked to write another series of teen novels, and those twelve stories turned into the Sierra Jensen books. Writers are told to "write what you know," and in Portland I began to know a lot about daffodils, rain-streaked windows, and the friendships between students at a private Christian school. What was consistently going on around us in life flowed into Sierra's stories. Rising at 3:00 a.m. three days each week continued to be my writing pattern.

The great thing with unhappy times is to take them bit by bit, hour by hour like an illness. It is seldom the present, the exact present, that is unbearable.
—*C. S. Lewis, Letters to an American Lady*

The banner word for my writing became *consistency*.

If I didn't spend time each day eating up the truths in God's Word, my wayward spirit would find lots of unhealthy thoughts and fears to devour. If I wasn't praying consistently and surrendering each moment to my Savior, my heart would sprout feet and run to a crazy-making place in my head that was like a theme park for worrywarts. Fretting was the spinning teacups ride. Round and round I'd go without getting anywhere. Fear was the great rising and plunging monster roller coaster. Anxiety kept my thoughts going in dizzying loops on a Ferris wheel that never stopped.

The ticket that guaranteed my entrance to this theme park of terror was our financial situation. We had taken a big step moving to Portland so my husband could attend graduate school full-time. We weren't covered by health insurance at the time, so my unexpected surgery and extended hospital stay took an enormous financial toll. We emptied our savings account to cover the thousands of dollars owed in hospital and doctors' bills and resigned ourselves to the likelihood that we would never be able to buy a house. Worse than that, we weren't sure how we would keep up our rent payments.

But day by day, step by step, we faithfully did what was before us and trusted God to accomplish his purposes in our lives. And along the way, we discovered a great secret. God blesses grateful hearts. He places gifts into hands that are open to him. He desires that we trust him and thank him even before our prayers are answered. When we have everything we need in reach, we don't cry out to the Lord as Hannah did. We don't remember that we are dependent on him for every breath.

As we trusted our heavenly Father each day and sincerely thanked him even before he placed our daily bread in our hands, we found that our hearts, lives, and bellies were always full. We always had enough. Always. Even when it looked on paper as if we would come up short, every month we had enough.

Nothing in life was easy. But God was faithful.

Many mornings when my alarm went off at 3:00, I felt no motivation to get up and write. No burst of celestial energy made me want to roll out of bed and pick up a pen or put my fingers to the keyboard. I came to work each morning with no award-winning ideas brewing alongside my steeping pot of tea, no certainty of what should happen next in the story. All I could do was be consistent.

What good would it do to say, "One day I plan to write a book," unless I set my alarm, got up in those "cobwebby hours" of the morning, and actually started with chapter 1, page 1. Small beginnings are good because they are a beginning.

Do not despise these small beginnings, for the LORD *rejoices to see the work begin.*

—Zechariah 4:10 NLT

As I sought to be consistent in my writing and my relationship with God, I discovered more of his grace. I had first seen God's grace as a gift of unmerited favor, like the lavish grace he poured out on Hannah in granting her request for a child. I had also learned that grace is a protective covering God places over us, like the covering of animal skins he gave to Eve in an act of reconciling grace and love. Now, in these early morning hours, I discovered that grace is also the source of our strength. By his Spirit, God empowers us to exercise the discipline and consistency necessary to live out his plans for our lives. He had given me the opportunity to write for teens, and through his grace, he would also give me the discipline I needed to do the work.

It is good for our hearts to be strengthened by grace.

—Hebrews 13:9

One day an editor from a publishing house contacted me. The publisher had taken note of the Christy Miller and Sierra Jensen series and wanted to know if I would be interested in writing novels as part of a new line of pure adult romances. This invitation caught me by surprise. I hadn't gone out searching for a new project or venue that would net a bigger audience. In the midst of doing what I had been consistently doing for years, God brought a publisher to me.

That contract gave us the financial boost we needed to buy our house. The day we signed the escrow papers was a time of grand elation. God had made a way for us. He blessed us far above and beyond what we had hoped for—gazebo and all.

Before the carpet was laid, we went through our new home room by room with permanent markers and a Bible and performed a small ceremony of thanksgiving and remembrance. On the rough floor in every room, we wrote out a Bible verse as a way of marking our gratefulness to the Lord for his provision.

On the dining-room floor, where family and friends would one day gather around our table, we wrote Psalm 34:8: "Taste and see that the Lord is good." On the floor beneath our bed, my husband and I wrote Proverbs 3:24: "When you lie down, you will not be afraid; when you lie down, your sleep will be sweet."

Our daughter wrote Psalm 23:1 on the floor of her room: "The Lord is my shepherd. He gives me everything I need" (NIrV).

And in the room that would become my writing nest, I pressed the permanent marker to the rough wood floor and wrote the verse that had motivated me ten years earlier to keep writing when I wanted to give up: "Let this be written for a future generation, that a people not yet created may praise the LORD" (Psalm 102:18).

This ceremony was poignant for us as we recalled the ups and downs, triumphs and defeats we had gone through together. This house was a gift from the Lord, and he had included us in the blessing by inviting each of us to daily, consistently do what he had put before us, no matter how menial the task might seem. And faithfully, every day, he gave us the grace to obey.

I wondered if that might be another way God prepares us to be his victims of grace. Second Chronicles 16:9 says, "The eyes of the LORD search the whole earth in order to strengthen those whose hearts are fully committed to him" (NLT). Our part in the blessing is to be committed to him and faithful in doing whatever work he puts in our path.

Yet God does more than just measure out a blessing for our faithfulness. The blessing happens inside our obedience. And inside the blessing, he delights in adding a hidden sweetness. That sweetness is love.

A Kindred Victim of Grace

That was how it happened for Rebekah. She rose one morning, like every other morning, and went about her tasks with consistency and kindness. But by the time she put her head on her pillow that night, everything had changed.

It had been more than two thousand years since Adam and Eve were banished from the garden of Eden. A vast span of years during which God's rebellious children had repeatedly broken his heart.

Rebekah lived in the same corner of the world in which Eve first stepped out from under the covering of consistent communion with the Father. Rebekah's home was in the same region where, after the fall, Eve experienced the new truth that everything in life was hard. Adam tilled the soil. Eve travailed in great pain during childbirth. Yet they were victims of grace, and that grace caused the soil to bear fruit. That grace gave Eve a song to hum in the night as she rocked her babies.

Rebekah was a kindred victim of that grace. And inside her story is the hidden sweetness of love.

On an ordinary day, in the cool of the evening, Rebekah went with the women of the town to draw water from the community well. It was a common task that required consistency. Kindness and a good attitude were optional, but what a grand thing it was that Rebekah had both.

When she arrived at the well, a traveler from a distant land was waiting. He had been sent on a journey of more than five hundred miles to find just the right woman for his master's son. His master was Abraham, the patriarch whom God called his friend. How extraordinary it must have been to be called God's friend. Abraham had a son named Isaac who had been God's gift in Abraham and Sarah's old age. And now Isaac was ready—more than ready—to take a wife and see the birth of his own sons.

When Abraham gave his servant orders to return to the land of Abraham's birth to obtain a bride for Isaac, the servant had asked Abraham how he would find this very special woman. Abraham told him, "[God] will send his angel before you so that you can get a wife for my son from there" (Genesis 24:7).

Talk about a match made in heaven!

The servant took his mission seriously. He journeyed over rough terrain, and when he arrived in his master's homeland, he asked the God of Abraham to direct him and give him success that day. Then he prayed for a sign: "May it be that when I say to a young woman, 'Please let down your jar that I may have a drink,' and she says, 'Drink, and I'll water your camels too'—let her be the one you have chosen for your servant Isaac" (verse 14).

This was quite a request. Yet before he had even finished praying, he looked up and saw Rebekah coming toward him with a water jug on her shoulder. She was "very beautiful, a virgin" who was old enough to marry (verse 16). The servant watched Rebekah fill her jar; then he put his prayer to the test, running over to her and asking for a drink of water.

Rebekah responded with extravagant graciousness. She gave Abraham's servant a drink, not knowing who he was or why he was there. Then she did exactly what the servant had prayed for: she offered to water all his camels. The account says that "she quickly emptied her jar into the trough" and "ran back to the well to draw more water" (verse 20). This meant she had to run back and forth from the well to the trough until she had watered all his camels. What a woman!

Let's do the math. The servant had ten camels. If those camels had been drained dry on their five-hundred-mile journey, each camel would drink around fifteen gallons of water. Rebekah offered to water the camels "until they have finished drinking" (verse 19 NASB). That could have been a total of 150 gallons of water.

Think about the last time you carried just a single gallon-sized jug of milk from the car to your kitchen. Imagine repeating that task 150 times, running back and forth to complete the task as "quickly" as possible. Now imagine doing that for a stranger, or more accurately, doing that sort of hard labor for a stranger's camels—stinky, spitting, ungrateful camels.

Rebekah offered to serve in this kind way, and she did it without any hint from the servant that she might be rewarded for her work. She could have quit at any time. Who would have blamed her for doing as much as she could manage and then stopping when the work became too exhausting?

The account in Genesis 24 makes it clear that she completed the task swiftly, and apparently without any complaints or excuses. That's extraordinary!

After Rebekah had kept her word and finished the work, the servant presented her with a gift to show his appreciation: two gold bracelets and a gold nose ring. He then discovered that Rebekah was part of the family line from which his master had directed him to select a wife for Isaac. The Lord had answered the servant's prayer and had indeed given him success that day.

How did the servant respond? Did he jump up and down with joy? Did he spill the details to Rebekah? Did he pat himself on the back? No. His reaction was weighted with the stuff of eternal blessings.

The servant bowed down and worshipped the Lord, saying, "Praise be to the LORD, the God of my master Abraham" (verse 27).

Rebekah's selfless act of service caused an observer to stop and worship God. The praise was offered not to Rebekah but to the Lord, the One who deserves all glory, honor, and praise.

This was a hidden sweetness tucked into the blessing born of faithfulness. When least expected, evidence of God's plan was revealed, even on an ordinary day in the midst of a menial task performed consistently and faithfully. Something as dreary and demanding as watering livestock turned into a pivotal moment when the life of a faithful young woman was changed forever.

When Rebekah got up that morning, everything was the same as it had always been. But by the time she put her head on her pillow that night, everything in her life had changed.

What happened after the camel watering? Abraham's servant was taken to meet Rebekah's family, and in their presence he told the story, scene by scene, line by line. He didn't leave out a detail. And neither did God when he recorded the story in his Book, so that it could be recounted for hundreds of generations. Rebekah's faithful efforts in the most mundane of tasks didn't go unnoticed.

The servant invited Rebekah to return with him to his master's land and give herself in marriage to a man she had never met. Rebekah could have delayed her decision. She could have said no. The servant could have sought another woman to marry Isaac, and if no one was willing, he would have been released from his vow.

But Rebekah didn't hesitate. She agreed to leave everything and go with Abraham's servant on one very long, bumpy, and dusty journey into an unknown future. Could it be that she recognized God's fingerprints all over this encounter? Is it possible that God had planted his dreams in her heart? Had she spent many starry nights dreaming of the man she might one day marry and wondering why she longed for something more than the life she had known?

The next scene recorded for us in God's Book of true stories is the moment when Isaac and Rebekah first laid eyes on each other. Try to picture the moment. Have you ever seen a field of wheat or barley at twilight? Have you seen how the amber shades of sunset can stream between the shafts of grain and set the field aflame with golden light? The sky softens to a faint shade of lavender. A flock of brown starlings quickly rises and takes flight, first right and then left, writing a sonnet in the sky.

I picture such a scene when Isaac was out walking in the field, meditating in the cool of the evening. I don't know whether there was a lavender sky or a flock of starlings, but I'd like to think so. That's why I hope we get to watch reruns in heaven. I'd love to watch this story on a celestial screen.

Can you imagine the expression on Isaac's face when he looked up and realized that the caravan coming toward him was his father's? The servant had returned at long last with all ten camels and … a woman! Yes, there definitely was a woman riding on one of the camels. The woman who was about to become Isaac's bride.

Rebekah noticed Isaac too. She saw him coming toward them while they were still a distance away. Quickly dismounting from her camel, Rebekah asked the servant, "Who is that man walking through the fields to meet us?" (verse 65 NLT).

I wonder. Was Isaac approaching them with decisive strides, or were his steps measured and cautious? He had many days to ponder his father's decision to send the servant in search of a bride. Did Isaac trust his father and the servant? Did Isaac believe the endeavor would have a beneficial conclusion for him?

Or did Isaac simply entrust the matter to God alone? Did he believe, as David wrote in Psalm 23 and our daughter penned on her bedroom floor thousands of years later, "The LORD is my shepherd. He gives me everything I need" (Psalm 23:1 NIrV)? Isaac's faith had been tried at a young age, when he journeyed with his father for three days to Mount Moriah. Isaac knew the purpose of the journey was to offer a sacrifice. He was the one carrying the wood. His father was carrying the fire and the knife. Yet something was missing. Oh yes, the lamb.

Abraham told Isaac that God himself would provide the sacrifice for the burnt offering. God did indeed provide the sacrifice—a ram caught in the bushes. But the ram didn't appear until after Abraham had bound Isaac and had given every indication that he would offer up the son he loved as the required sacrifice.

Did Isaac extrapolate from that experience the belief that God could be trusted? Did he place his faith not in his father, or in his father's servant, but in God alone? If he did, then his heart must have been filled with expectation and confidence as he walked through the golden field to meet his bride.

As directed by her culture and tradition, Rebekah covered her face with a veil when Isaac approached. The two of them stood in each other's presence, and the servant once again told the story, no doubt line by line, leaving out nothing, making it clear these events hadn't happened by chance. The God of Abraham had directed the servant's steps and answered his prayers.

Did Isaac gaze on Rebekah as the tale of her deeds was told? Did his heart pound when she glanced at him from behind her veil? Not much of their love story is recorded from that moment on. We are given only this: "She became his wife. Isaac loved her very much" (Genesis 24:67 NCV).

There it is! The love. Very much love. The blessing happened inside the obedience, and the sweetness inside the blessing was love. Isaac loved Rebekah very much.

None of the other patriarchs in Genesis has this sort of "and they lived happily ever after" line added to their stories. The Bible is brimming with tales of faithfulness and unfaithfulness, marriages and broken hearts, pregnancies and barrenness, life and death. But only in Isaac and Rebekah's tale do we read, "Isaac loved her very much."

When Rebekah agreed to this arranged marriage, did she have any hope of being loved? Any dream of being loved "very much"? Or did she simply take the first step in obedience and find herself surprised at the blessing hidden inside that obedience?

Whether she realized it or not, Rebekah was a victim of grace.

The Relentless Lover

Soon after my first pure romance novel was released, the publisher scheduled a live interview for me. Once again I entered a building in downtown Portland in broad daylight. But this time the building was a radio station, and I was fully aware of everything that was going on.

I was led down a hallway to a studio sound booth, where a commercial was playing over the sound system. The radio host pointed to the headset and microphone waiting for me. I got set up as quickly and quietly as possible and then waited for the signal that we were back on the air, live.

When the show resumed, the host leaned into the microphone and, in a mesmerizing tone, introduced me as the in-studio guest that afternoon.

Turning to me, he said, "So, my first question for you is, how can you call yourself a Christian and write romance novels?"

I hadn't done a lot of radio interviews and wasn't sure how to reply. His tone was accusatory.

So the words that tumbled out of my mouth weren't premeditated. "I guess I would have to say the reason is because I know that a true love story can change your life."

"What do you mean by that?" His head was tilted, and his eyes had narrowed.

"Well, when I was a teenager, I read a love story that changed my life. It starts off great, but then right away everything falls apart. The Relentless Lover in the story wants his first love to come back to him, but she resists for years."

The host gave a nod, indicating that I should continue.

"Then, three-fourths of the way through the book, he does everything he can to prove his love to her and persuade her to be his bride, but she's still rebellious. Finally, in the last chapter, he comes riding in on a white horse and takes her away to be with him forever."

"And how did a story like that change your life?" the host asked. "It sounds like a formula romance to me."

"Really? Because I was talking about the Bible. There's a white horse and everything. We're even called the bride of Christ."

For a moment we had something no radio host ever wants during a program—dead air.

Then he sat back and gave me a half grin. "You're right. I never saw it that way before. The Bible is the ultimate love story, isn't it?"

I nodded and then realized that the radio listeners couldn't see my nod, so I added, "Yes. Absolutely. That's why I see God as the Relentless Lover. For a thousand generations he will never stop pursuing us, because he wants us back."

What followed after that was a lively interview in which I brought up Isaac and Rebekah's love story. I'm sure my thoughts about them weren't new or original. "There is nothing new under the sun," as Solomon said in Ecclesiastes 1:9.

Isaac and Rebekah's love story draws out such a lovely analogy of God's dream that will one day be fulfilled. Abraham, the father in the love story, resembles God the Father. Isaac, the son whom Abraham was willing to sacrifice, echoes what happened when God sacrificed his only Son, Jesus.

And we are Rebekah in the story. We have choices every day as to how we will go about the tasks set before us. We choose whether to be generous and kind in what we do. It has been that way for millennia. God notices and rewards consistency and obedience, even when no one else is looking.

One day everything will change. Just as Abraham sent his servant on a journey to find a bride for his son Isaac, our heavenly Father has sent the Holy Spirit on a mission to woo us, give us gifts, and invite us to become the bride of Christ.

Yet the choice is still with us. Will we say yes, or will we hold on to all that is familiar and stay behind in the place of broken communion with God? Or Rebekah-like, will we say yes and let the Holy Spirit lead us on a bumpy journey into an unknown future?

To add further sweetness hidden inside this story, think of how it was when at last Isaac and Rebekah met face-to-face. Isaac wasn't at home in his father's dwelling, amid all of his father's wealth, when he and Rebekah met. No, Isaac had left his father's home and was in the middle of a field between his bride and the place he had prepared for her.

What a thrilling foreshadowing that is of how the return of our Bridegroom will be! One day we, the bride of Christ, will be on our long, dusty journey through life, and in an instant, Jesus, our Bridegroom, will be there, coming in the clouds, coming to claim us. Our Prince of Peace will take us to the place he has made ready for us.

And there he will love us very much.

A Trip to England

One day, like any other day, as I was writing chapter after chapter of pure romance for the Glenbrooke series, God infused the consistency of my work with a sudden sweetness. An unexpected gift of his opulent love. A sweetness that he knew would be my favorite flavor. I was invited to go on a trip!

The president of Media Associates International (MAI) invited me to teach a workshop at the LittWorld international writers' conference. That in and of itself was exciting and honoring. For many years, this global ministry had provided on-site training for writers and publishers in difficult places in the world. The sweetness God added to that blessing was that this conference was being held in England, a place I dearly love.

It had been almost twenty-five years since my summer trip to Europe as a college student. And nearly that many years since I'd been turned down as a laundry supervisor in Africa. During all that time, I had been doing the work God placed in front of me, the good work of loving my husband and children. I'd been faithfully writing, striving to remain consistent, not daring to dream that I would ever see more of God's wide world.

If I'd been asked to teach a workshop at any other writers' conference, I would have been thrilled. I vividly remembered my first writers' conference and considered it a privilege to be the sort of catalyst and encourager that authors like Ethel Herr had been to me in my formative writing years. The fact that the conference was to be held in England, though, was God's gift of hidden sweetness.

I couldn't help but wonder why we so often insist on formulating our own dreams and then demand that God fulfill them. It's as if we take credit for the passion that has long brewed inside us, usurping the position of Director of Dreams and demanding favors from God. Or worse, we allow the wickedness of entitlement to seep in, believing we deserve whatever we want because God owes us. In our prayers, we become brassy adolescents, pointing our fingers at God and demanding that he make good on his promises.

How much sweeter to receive his gifts freely and unexpectedly.

What an eye-opener to us and those around us when, right in the middle of our consistency in the ordinariness of everyday life, he fulfills a desire he planted in our hearts long ago.

I packed my bags and headed for England. The flight was long. The November weather was dreary. My roommate, Anne, was an American who had made the Netherlands her home when she married a Dutchman. She had recently been in Africa and spent several days in our room, alternating between shivers and terrible sweats as she rode out a bout of malaria. Nothing about the conference was as enchanting as I had imagined it would be.

All my long-held, fanciful notions of life on the mission field were radically altered as, over dinner, I talked with writers from around the world and heard about the hardships they faced. How naive I had been to picture life in other parts of the world as more fulfilling and exciting than what I knew in the United States. I thought the rural simplicity would activate a deeper joy and initiate a stronger love for the Lord. I pictured people from less developed corners of the globe being happier than materialistic Westerners.

What I discovered is that life is difficult everywhere.

Some of the conferees I met told of how they had been persecuted for writing and publishing Christian materials. Some of them wrote under a pseudonym and had their work published in such a way that couldn't be traced back to them or put their families in jeopardy.

One highly educated man who held a significant position in his country published his testimony, and as a result, the government came after him. He and his family had managed to flee in time and now lived in a different country.

This wasn't the sort of writing life I was living. The cumulative revenue from their books would rarely, if ever, be enough for a down payment on a house. In the writing world I lived in, banquets were held and awards were given out. Best-selling authors bought homes with their earnings while these fellow writers in difficult places around the world penned their words at the kitchen table late at night, with all the shades drawn so their neighbors wouldn't discover what they were doing and report their subversive activities to the authorities.

As I listened to the stories of these brothers and sisters in Christ, I thought of Isaac and Rebekah's story. These writers were like Rebekah, tirelessly and faithfully doing the hard work of writing with consistency, strength, and courage. Like Rebekah, they were generous, and many of them had amazingly positive attitudes. They were strong. They were willing. They were faithful. But they had yet to see any reward for their labor.

Like the servant, I was the one who was humbled and awed by God's grace. I had come a long way to gather with these authors at this well of writing. My small sacrifice was nothing compared to theirs. Just being around them was humbling. Like Abraham's servant, all I could do was bow my heart and worship God for his kindness and faithfulness.

At lunch one day I sat beside a woman named Wambura, who told me she was familiar with the Christy Miller books. When she was in high school, she and other girls at her school had read them.

Her accent sounded British to me, but her skin and mannerisms reflected a more exotic homeland. So I had to ask her, "Wambura, where are you from?"

"Nairobi, Kenya. It's in East Africa."

"Yes," I said, as an old familiar *tha-thump* quickened my heart. "I know exactly where Nairobi is. When I was about your age, I thought I was going to Nairobi. I applied for a position with a mission there."

"And what was the position?"

"Laundry supervisor."

"Is that so?" She seemed to be holding back her mirth.

I didn't hold back. I laughed and told her how I thought I was going to put a big basket on my head and traipse down to the river, where I would pound the dirt out of clothes with only a rock and my bare hands. I even added the part about singing with the other women as we worked side by side and the babies splashed in the river. And of course, there would be elephants.

She laughed with me.

"But I never went." My chin dipped with regret. "I was rejected as a laundry supervisor, so I never made it to Kenya."

"Ah, but your stories came to Africa."

I lifted my eyes to meet Wambura's encouraging gaze. "Perhaps you were never supposed to come," she said. "That wasn't part of the plan God had for you. Only your stories were supposed to come. They were the real missionaries. Don't you see?"

I let her words sink deep into the part of my heart that still felt a twinge of shame and regret over never becoming a missionary.

Wambura gently touched my arm. "Robin, you did not need to come to Africa to wash our laundry. You sent your stories, and they have washed our hearts."

I held my breath at the impact of her words. God had not sent me to Africa. He sent my stories instead. And in that moment, looking into Wambura's face and listening to her voice, he had brought Africa to me.

But as it is written:
"Eye has not seen,
nor ear heard,
Nor have entered into
the heart of man
The things which God
has prepared for those
who love Him."
—1 Corinthians 2:9 NKJV

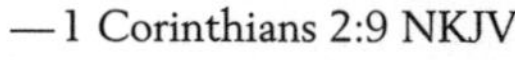

Wambura headed out for the next workshop while I sat alone for a few moments in the dining room. My mind was trying to take in the unexpected aerial view God had just given me of his big-picture plan for my life. He'd gifted me to tell stories. As I had been responsive to that gifting and faithful to the calling over the years, he had fulfilled the missionary-woman dream of my heart. My stories had gone around the world to places I would never go. The characters in those stories were telling thousands of readers about God's love and they were responding.

It was such a bigger dream than I had ever dared to dream.

That's when I realized that in the next season of my life, God's plan had not been to nullify the old dream and replace it with a new dream. No. It was all the same dream. He had been accomplishing his purposes for me from the very beginning. Just not in the way I had expected.

Oh, the enormous, unimagined, magnificent ways of God!

Now the question that laced my prayers was, "What's next, Lord?" The treasure hunt to find the big picture of his plan had begun.

Chapter 5

MAKING PEACE WITH THE MYSTERIES

I will give you treasures hidden in the darkness—
secret riches. I will do this so you may know
that I am the Lord, *the God of Israel,*
the one who calls you by name.

—Isaiah 45:3 NLT

The trip I had taken to England to teach a workshop at the writers' conference had opened the door to more opportunities for international travel, including trips to Finland and Latvia. God was accomplishing his purposes for me. He was fulfilling my dream of traveling around the world and telling people about his love. Just as Wambura had pointed out so cleverly, God was sending the stories to places I would never go.

My dad loved the stories I told about my overseas travels. I loved that as I told him these stories, every word was true. Nothing was made up the way my stories used to be when I got in trouble at the dinner table for "exaggerating" and "going on and on about nothing." Jesus, the

Author and Finisher of my faith as he is called in Hebrews 12, truly had redeemed the hidden gift he had placed inside me before I was even born. He gave me the gift, he redeemed the gift, and now he was using that gift to reveal his Great Story to others.

Telling my father the stories of my travels was one special way we connected during the final chapter of his life. Years earlier, on a normal Tuesday afternoon, I had called my parents to catch up. The conversation was short, not much to say. Kids are fine. All is well. Talk to you later. Bye.

Two days later, on Thursday, my father had a stroke. It was the first of several TIAs, followed by a brain-stem stroke that paralyzed him on the right side and stole his ability to speak. Strange guttural sounds came out of his mouth instead of well-shaped words. In his clear blue eyes, we could read the terror of what had happened. In his brain he knew what he was trying to say. His thoughts were still all there. The stroke hadn't taken his ability to think, but it had robbed him of the ability to express his thoughts.

> The imagination, like all our faculties, has participated in the Fall. But just as we can believe that God can take our reason (fallen as it is) and sanctify it and use if for his good purposes, so we believe he can sanctify the imagination and use *it* for his good purposes.
>
> —*Richard J. Foster, Celebration of Discipline*

He was a prisoner in his own body and remained that way for the next five and a half years.

What a severe suspension of life it was. My father had been active his entire life. The man was a mule. He had taught physical education in the Irvine, California, school district for more than thirty-five years. During the summers he backpacked in the mountains surrounding Mammoth Lakes. After he retired, he signed up for several missions trips, including one to Ecuador, where he carried wood, swung a hammer, and helped to build a school. Nothing in my father's demeanor prepared him to be a passive invalid.

Why would God allow such a thing to happen to such a person? It made no sense.

Each time we visited my father at home, where my mom faithfully cared for him, we'd practice learning a new language. The vocabulary was Dad's own creation and involved the use of eyebrows, sounds of various tones all caught in the throat, and lots of pointing with the thick finger on his one good hand. Every now and then, a complete word or phrase would escape his lips as if the drawbridge from his brain to his mouth had unexpectedly lowered, allowing a rush of thoughts. Then, just as quickly as the drawbridge had been let down, it snapped back up nice and tight, and he would fall into an exhausted sleep.

Like most men from my father's generation, gruffness was standard. Firm expressions of discipline were mandatory. He rarely talked about his overseas term of duty during World War II, but whenever the subject floated into the room, it seemed to cover his handsome face with a shadow, a reminder of atrocities seen and sorrows buried deep inside when his soul was young.

Growing up, my sister, brother, and I knew our father loved us. But instead of speaking the words, he demonstrated his love by providing for our family. Of course we would have liked to hear those words during our childhoods. And we wished that our father had been more affirming and supportive of our life choices. But we were an average family, and our dad was like everyone else's dad, except that he had a witty sense of humor.

But during the five and a half years my dad tarried on this earth after his stroke, God blessed us with a special gift. Nothing will ever compare to the treasure we received during that dark time. We got to hear our father tell us he loved us. The words came out with great effort and in a tightened gurgle, but we knew what "Ahh wuv uu" meant. We snatched those three sounds and deposited them in our hearts as if they were gold coins.

On numerous occasions, with his grandchildren and all three of us grown children, my dad would take our hands in his and lift them so he could plant a crooked, misshapen kiss on our knuckles. Every time that sacred blessing was given, we would get teary-eyed and receive it deep in our souls, which carried the wounds from our youth. On each visit, our invisible treasure chest grew fuller and fuller.

Our father had turned into a softie. His eyes would light up when we entered his bedroom and elevated his hospital bed. He would follow us with his stiffened neck, eyebrows raised, waiting for a story, eager to hear some news.

One of the stories my dad seemed to like hearing again and again was about the trip I had taken to Finland and Latvia. The Christy Miller books had been translated into Finnish, and the publisher had invited me to speak to the teenagers in a few churches outside Helsinki and in several public schools. I think one of the things my dad liked hearing about was the freedom I had to openly share my faith in Finnish public schools.

My time in Latvia was the other part of the story that made my dad's eyes narrow and focus on me more intently. My friend Donna had accompanied me on the grand adventure. She had friends who were serving in ministry in Riga, Latvia's capital city. Since Riga is only a hop across the Baltic Sea from Helsinki, we stuffed our suitcases with American goodies, such as chocolate chips and marionberry jam from Oregon, and paid them a visit.

While Donna and I were in Latvia, our interpreter asked if we would consider visiting an invalid named Mary.

I looked at Donna. She looked at me. After an already intense day, we were exhausted. We had spent the day sharing our hearts, teaching from the Bible, and standing for hours listening through an interpreter to dozens of hurting women as they looked to us for any morsel of encouragement we could offer. Now I was ready to find a few nourishing morsels of food before falling into the nearest bed. Offering my weary self to all the germs in the presence of an ill person seemed like a bad idea.

"It's up to you." Donna gave me a bedraggled look.

Apparently it wasn't truly up to me, because even though my mind was saying "Sorry, no," my mouth somehow interpreted those two simple words into "Okay, we'll go." What is it the Bible says about the Spirit of God interceding for us? Does he translate our intentions as well?

By the time we left the church that evening, it was after nine o'clock. We had been graciously offered a ride to Mary's house so we wouldn't have to depend on the public tram. But in this case, the hospitality offered exceeded the maximum load capacity available. Like a troop of circus clowns, we smushed six bodies into a tiny sedan built for four bodies.

> We have to learn to interpret the mysteries of life in the light of our knowledge of God. Until we can come face to face with the deepest, darkest fact of life without damaging our view of God's character, we do not yet know Him.
>
> —*Oswald Chambers, My Utmost for His Highest*

Our ten-minute ride turned into twenty minutes. I felt as if we were being kidnapped. The dark skies suddenly hurled javelins of lightning followed by roars of thunder as we pulled up in front of a dilapidated manor. Big drops of rain pelted us as we performed a series of unattractive contortions to extract our bodies from the car. I opened my travel umbrella, but a gust of wind popped it inside out. Nothing about that moment felt good.

We dashed to the front door, where a flickering overhead light welcomed us. Mary's full-time caregiver invited us inside and ushered us quietly into what had once been the dining room of this large house. In typical Communist fashion, the upstairs and downstairs had been converted into many cubicles, and a separate family now occupied each cubicle.

Tentatively approaching the corner where a single lamp was lit, we came as close as we dared to the narrow bed where the diminished invalid sat, propped up by a pillow. Her white hair was clean and combed back from her glowing face. I didn't expect Mary to be so astonishingly beautiful.

At first I wondered if the dim light on this elderly woman's pale skin gave her such a glow. Or did she have a fever—a contagious sort of fever that made her look rosy and vital when she actually was oh so infectious?

She stretched out her right hand, eager to greet us, to touch us. Her fingers curled in, her wrist was bent. Yet she smiled radiantly. Donna and I hung back, waving our hellos rather than making contact with her. Then I noticed that Mary had no lumps under the covers where her legs should have been. Her left hand lay motionless at her side.

Mary wasn't contagiously sick. She had contracted polio forty years before, when part of the remedy included amputation.

Donna and I were offered two of the three wobbly, straight-backed chairs available. Mary began at once to roll out her story for us. Our interpreter could barely keep up as Mary described her losses: a baby at birth, another child in his toddler years, and her husband soon after he was drafted into the USSR army. By the time she was twenty-two, Mary had lost everything. Then the polio came and took her legs.

The demure woman spoke softly, with her chin down, as she described how angry she had been with God and how deep the darkness had been that swallowed her for several years. Then she asked God a question. Not a "why" question but a "what" question. "What can I possibly do for you now? I am of no use."

And God answered her.

"God told me he took my legs so I would not run around on this earth," Mary said. "Nearly anyone can do that. He asked me to do something different for him. Something special. Something not everyone can do. He asked me to run every day between this earth and heaven and carry up to him the heart cries of his children. This is my job. My purpose. I run to heaven every day."

I blinked back the tears and found it easy to believe that every time Mary stepped into those courts of heaven, she returned to earth with a bit of glory dust on her face. That was why she glowed.

Our interpreter went on to add that Mary used her one crippled hand to write letters to encourage believers around the world, since she knew what it was like to be swallowed by deep darkness. She understood how susceptible they were to discouragement and despair. Mary's eyes shone when she told us she wrote to Corrie ten Boom once, and Corrie, via an interpreter, wrote her back.

Mary pulled a crumpled envelope from under her pillow and showed the letter to us. The letter had been mailed from the same California office where I had worked so many years ago. It was entirely possible that I was the assistant who folded this very letter and placed it in the envelope Mary now held in her frail grasp. As I told her about meeting Corrie, Mary cried. I went on to tell her how Corrie's life and books had inspired me to serve the Lord when I was a young woman.

Then I told her about a children's book I'd written called *Mrs. Rosey Posey and the Fine China Plate.* I'd read it to the children at church just that morning and happened to have a copy in my shoulder bag. I told Mary how Mrs. Rosey Posey was modeled after Tante Corrie, and then, with the translator's help, I read the story to Mary. She beamed at the end, with tears in her eyes, as I closed the book and told her, "Mary, you have been set apart, just like a fine china plate. The Lord is using you to serve others."

It was a moment of full circles.

Donna and I were reluctant to leave as we leaned close to Mary and said our good-byes. We curled our arms around her and pressed our cheeks against hers, leaving kisses in the tears that continued to flow down her rosy, glowing face. As we parted, she promised us something very special: she promised to pray for Donna and me every day. And I believe she did.

One November morning two years after our visit on that stormy night, Mary made her daily run to heaven, but this time Jesus told her she could stay.

My dad loved this story, and both of us knew without exchanging any words that one of these quiet mornings, Jesus would come for him. The atrophied legs and feet I rubbed as I told him Mary's story would be restored, and he would go jogging again. Only this time it would be on streets of gold.

The Terrible Power of "What If?"

During this season of my life, I had no idea how vulnerable I was. Everything seemed to heighten my emotions. The highs were unusually high, and the lows were disparaging. I didn't see it happening at first, but a subtle wearing-away of my spirit was taking place, and it was pressing against my marriage.

I believed from the moment when I said "I do" that nothing could cause me to leave the covenant commitment I made to my husband. We had weathered terrible times in our early years. We had fought against each other and against forces that weren't flesh and blood but were powers and principalities of darkness. We had made it through every time. We were a team. We were strong, and together we were seeing our dreams come true for our family.

My husband and I were more than two decades into our relationship when I found myself crying in secret and feeling overwhelmed by a weighty sense of discontent that had covered my life like a leaden apron worn in the dentist's chair. Was what I was feeling hormonal? Was it spiritual warfare? Was I feeding on the poisonous fruit of my sin nature? Did my dad's debilitating situation and the regular trips to California play a hand?

All I knew was that I was sad for many weeks.

At just the right time, an old love interest from college days slipped back into my life, and I felt happy—skip-a-heartbeat happy—when he took a keen interest in me. He praised my writing. He sympathized with all that we were going through and said things that made me nod my head and think, *Yes, you understand, don't you? You really see what I'm going through. I don't think my husband has ever fully understood these things about me that you name so effortlessly.*

On a particularly dreary, stressful day, I did something I never thought I would do.

I left my husband.

Not physically. I was still there, in the house God had provided, with the verses written by my own hand on the floors under the carpet. I was still there for our children and fully engaged in their teenage lives. I slept beside my husband. I kissed him and told him I loved him. But in my heart I was gone. I had made a clandestine departure emotionally, and I don't think he even knew it, since so many other factors could have explained my highs and lows.

When you have become full and prosperous and have built fine homes to live in, and when your flocks and herds have become very large and your silver and gold have multiplied along with everything else, be careful! Do not become proud at that time and forget the L*ORD your God, who rescued you.*

—Deuteronomy 8:12–14 NLT

I wasn't about to replace my husband with the old love interest who had resurfaced. That brief reconnection was only the catalyst that made me wonder what my life would be like if I replaced the present reality of "what is" with the fantasy of "what could be."

By opening my thoughts to what could be, I had marched into the garden of my heart and tossed out a handful of what-if possibilities, and they immediately sprouted. What would my life be like if I was no longer married? Would another man pursue me? The vagrant thoughts grew at a frenzied speed. I helped by watering them with every slight infraction my husband committed. If he became upset about something, forgot something, or irritated me in any way, I added that offense to the list.

You know the list. Before you're married, the list is all about every charming characteristic and attribute you want your future husband to come to the altar with. After you're married, the list is about every way your husband has failed to live up to the first list. The lists are unfair. I would never want someone to create either sort of list about me. Yet I had so easily strayed from the greatest commandment of loving God and loving the person closest to me, my neighbor, in the same way I wanted to be loved.

Selfish thoughts are like sunflowers once they take root. Up, up, up they go, and suddenly they are bright, beautiful, and bold. They demand our immediate attention and make it impossible for anything else to grow under their shadow.

Like brassy sunflowers in their summer prime, egotistical dreams burst with hundreds of potent seeds that quickly grow into more overpowering sunflowers. They rob the slumbering tulip bulbs of the elements they need to come up in their proper season. The sunflowers choke out and uproot the delicate ground cover that was intended to spread a cloak of beauty over the ashes and dirt.

So it was in my heart's garden. The question bound up in all those seeds that I scattered around in my thoughts was as old as Eden: What if?

The serpent beguiled Eve with the unspoken question, *What if you took this fruit and ate it?* Eve did, and she found out the consequences.

For me the beguiling questions were *What if I married the wrong man? What if I would be happier spending the rest of my days with someone else? What if I fled?*

One night I awoke with my heart racing. In our darkened bedroom, all I could see was an image of my heart's garden. It was overrun with sunflowers of self-absorbed possibilities. Why did they have to appear so stunningly inviting?

I padded downstairs to the living room and penned these words in my journal:

What never was, but might have been
What could have happened?
Would it be sin
To grasp this dangling thread so willing to be caught
And let it unravel the fantasies I've fought?

I knew the answer and yet I felt powerless to make the haunting nudges go away. Life seemed to hold so many possibilities that I'd never considered before. I finally couldn't take the conflict in my spirit any longer. I went to my friend Donna and honestly confessed my thoughts. I told her how unhappy and confused I felt.

Donna listened as I poured out my discontent. She knew. She understood. She felt for me. But she loved me too much to let me believe the lies. She could see what I couldn't see in that beguiling place. I had been deceived.

At last I asked her what she thought. With fire in her eyes she said, "Don't you dare leave your marriage. Do you hear me? If you do, so help me, I'll never get over it. I'll never recover from you, of all people, giving in to such a stupid lie. You know better. Stop what you're thinking right now and don't give way to this again. Ever!"

She then placed in my hands the equivalent of an invisible garden hoe and told me to uproot every one of those what-ifs. She spoke truth over me, telling me the place I belonged was inside my marriage. God's blessing would follow my obedience. I needed to get back under my husband's covering and not take off again into the wilderness of "if only." It didn't matter how difficult things were for me at home at that moment. That's where I belonged.

I returned home the long way that afternoon. As I drove I prayed and started the journey home in my heart. I had to tear down all the little shrines where I had worshipped myself and somehow come to believe that I was entitled to everything I desired in terms of happiness, thrills, and affirmation.

I chose to believe that my sin nature was no longer my master. I chose to put my spirit back under my husband's covering, which ultimately put me back under the great shadow of God's almighty canopy of grace. My spirit calmed.

Sin shall no longer be your master, because you are not under the law, but under grace.

—Romans 6:14

In the weeks that followed, the inklings and stirrings of unrest returned. I wanted to go back to that sunflower-infested garden the way an addict cycles back to her nemesis, convinced she needs a "fix" one more time. The entire affair had happened only in my mind. I had flirted with this emotional affair for such a short time, but whenever my thoughts returned to the "what if" question, the power of the unknown possibilities continued to grow monstrously strong.

To combat the onslaught, I copied 2 Corinthians 10:5 (NKJV) in my journal, and under it I wrote the date and these words:

Today I am casting down my imagination
And every high thing that exalts itself
Against the knowledge of God
And bringing into captivity
Every thought to the obedience of Christ.

Jesus said that if a man looks at a woman with lust in his heart, it's as if he has committed adultery with her. Is that any different from what I was doing, stepping out from under the covering of the vows I'd promised to keep when I stood before God and all those witnesses saying that I would love, honor, and cherish my husband "for richer or poorer, in sickness and in health, as long as we both shall live"?

I named the experience for what it was and brought it to the Lord with this prayer: "Father, forgive me for giving space in my thoughts to this emotional affair. 'Create in me a clean heart, O God, and renew a right spirit within me.' "

It was an important day. A day of vow renewals. Only this vow renewal didn't include a fancy dress and flowers, an audience and a cake; it was between the Prince of Peace, my true Bridegroom, and me. My sin was against him. And my vow renewal was with him.

Later that week, when the time was right, I told my husband what had been going on in my heart, and I asked him to forgive me. I remember feeling so vulnerable in that conversation. So human and so dearly in need of a Savior to redeem me and my wayward heart.

To his everlasting credit, my husband listened. He understood and forgave me, releasing me from a wrong that he could have held over me like a debt. I knew then, even more than I had realized before, that I had married the right man. An amazing man. By bringing everything out into the light, there was no room for lies to hide in the darkness.

My heart was clear, my marriage was stronger, and my feet were back on the straight and narrow path. In that darkened season God had given me hidden treasure and secret riches.

A Kindred Victim of Grace

I found a story in the Bible of another woman who left a difficult reality not because she was fiddling around with thoughts of infidelity but rather because she was mistreated. What happened to her was unfair. If any woman had a reason to give way to discontent and make a list of all she was entitled to, it was Hagar.

She was a servant from Egypt, and her mistress was Isaac's mother, Sarai. When Hagar's story appears in the Bible, Isaac had not yet been born, and therein lies the problem. God promised Abram that he would be the father of a great nation; yet he and Sarai had no children. Many years had passed since God had made his promise to Abram. So much waiting, but nothing had changed. Life wasn't getting better, nor was it moving forward.

That's when Sarai came up with her fast-growing, brazen sunflower of a solution. She was seventy-five years old, and Abram was eighty-five. Really, how were the two of them at this stage in life ever going to have a baby? It was laughable.

Sarai told Abram to take her maidservant Hagar and have a child through her. This solution wasn't absurd. It was customary at that time for a tribal head to have children through surrogate mothers when his own wife couldn't conceive.

Has that changed over the millennia? The main differences in our times might be the use of sterilized devices and the more impersonal way that the surrogate receives the seeds of human life. Although the methods may have differed, the concept was the same. In essence, Sarai said to Abram, "Here, I select this woman as the best option for a birth mother. Take her. Let her carry our child."

A short but telling phrase in Genesis 16:2 reveals what happened next: "Abram listened to the voice of Sarai" (NASB). I wonder what would have happened if he had listened to Sarai's heart instead of her voice. What was she feeling? As many women know so well, at times feelings overwhelm us, doing all the persuading and convincing over the voice of our logic. The "what if" questions take root and grow quickly. Our thoughts become polluted and what comes out of our mouth reflects it.

The voice of Sarai was very persuasive, it seems, because she convinced her husband to do as she proposed. Abram is one of the few people in history who had heard the Lord's voice. That was the voice Abram listened to when he was told he would have as many descendants as the sands on the seashore. But now he was listening to Sarai's voice. Was the message of the two voices consistent? Was this the Lord's doing all along? Was God using Sarai to announce his plan to Abram? Or was this another repercussion of the shattering that took place in the fall?

Whether the plan was God's first desire for Abram and Sarai or a symptom of the freewill that his omniscient grace allowed, the result was that Hagar conceived. When Sarai learned that Abram was going to have a child through the designated surrogate mother, it threw her into a tizzy.

Perhaps Sarai thought the infertility problem was with Abram and not with her. Or perhaps she thought Abram was just too old, and if he tried to have a child with Hagar and was as unsuccessful as he had been with Sarai, then it would be the end of the matter. Sarai wouldn't have to spend her old age watching as her dear husband's hopes were crushed by a dream that was never going to be.

The root of Sarai's thinking isn't made clear in their story, but what happens next is given to us in unvarnished fashion, as God does throughout his Book. God always tells his people's stories with honesty. He doesn't cover up or hide the facts or do a quick marketing fix so his patriarchs look better than they were.

This unmasked honesty is what gives each of us the freedom to tell our stories in the same way. We're troublemakers at heart. God knows that. He continues to demonstrate his eternal theme of grace in every real-life story in his Book, as well as in every generation. He makes it clear that each of us needs a Savior. Once we come to him, the process of sanctification begins, because with God, everything is redeemable.

In Sarai's story, the truth wasn't flattering. There she was, Abram's wife for decades. They had journeyed many hundreds of miles through innumerable obstacles. Their marriage

Remember the things
I have done in the past.
For I alone am God!
I am God, and there
is none like me.
Only I can tell you the future
before it even happens.
Everything I plan will come
to pass,
for I do whatever I wish.
—Isaiah 46:9–10 NLT

had weathered terrible storms. For years it had been asserted that she was the one who would become the mother of a great nation, because she was under her husband's covering. And yet she allowed space in her thoughts for a what-if plan. When the baby plan worked and "what could be" suddenly came true, Sarai blamed Abram. That's always the easiest first step. Adam blamed Eve. Eve blamed the serpent. Now Sarai blamed Abram.

If you took a moment to honestly ask, "Who have I blamed for the disappointments and times of lost hope in my life?" you might be surprised with the answer.

Abram directed Sarai to deal with Hagar as she saw fit, and Sarai took the opportunity to deal with Hagar "harshly" (Genesis 16:6 NASB). As a result, Hagar fled.

Pregnant and alone, Hagar wandered through the wilderness until she came to a spring. An angel of the Lord found her and asked, "Hagar, Sarai's maid, where have you come from, and where are you going?" (verse 8 NKJV).

Hagar answered honestly that she was fleeing from her mistress. She had taken herself out from under Sarai's covering and had taken matters into her own hands. She was seeking a different covering, a different life in which she would no longer be treated unfairly.

Hagar didn't answer the angel's second question. Maybe she didn't know where she was going. All she knew was that anything had to be better than where she had come from.

Most Bible commentators believe that the person who appeared to Hagar wasn't an angelic messenger like Gabriel but a *theophany*, a preincarnate appearance of God the Son. In other words, *Jesus* came to Hagar. He sought her, found her, and spoke her name. The question he asked Hagar was similar to the one God the Father asked Eve in Eden: "Where are you?"

Almost every time angelic messengers appear in the Bible, the first thing they say is, "Don't be afraid." That's not what the Lord said to

Hagar. Could it be that she wasn't afraid because she knew it was the Lord? He fit naturally in her surroundings.

When Jesus enters even the darkest seasons of our lives, he fits. He belongs in our surroundings quite naturally. We aren't afraid of him. He is accessible. We can speak with him.

The questions he asked Hagar weren't so different from the words Donna spoke to me when I fled to her house that day. It was as if he was telling her, "Stop. Look at where you've come from. Look at all that God has done for you. Now look at the future you are about to run headlong into. Consider what this really means."

Our Lord Jesus Christ and God our Father loved us. By his grace God gave us comfort that will last forever. The hope he gave us is good.

—2 Thessalonians 2:16 NIrV

Then the angel of the Lord told Hagar to return to Sarai. To place herself back under the covering of her mistress and submit to her. But with the command came a promise. His goodness would prevail. He promised to multiply her offspring through the son she would name Ishmael, so that her descendants would be too numerous to count.

Hagar did what the angel told her to do. She returned to Sarai.

After this experience, Hagar had a new name for the Lord. She called him "the One who sees me" (verse 13).

If you have ever been lost in a wilderness, treated unjustly, dealt with harshly, or have fled in fear or in the hope of something better, Hagar's story is for you. It is evidence of God's abiding grace, no matter what. You aren't alone. The Lord sees you. He hears. He knows. He is with you. His grace will comfort you.

It's not unusual to feel as if you are caught like a prisoner in your life. At times you may wonder if something or someone out there is better than what you have now. That's a common temptation for every human since the garden.

But is what you must endure right now unbearable? Deep down, if you're honest, you know that God is right there with you, even if your situation is uncomfortable, discouraging, or unfair. He is accomplishing his plan for you. His comfort is available. His hope is good.

Even in the confines of your situation, an abiding grace resides. This grace brings comfort and enables someone like Mary in Riga to be radiant as she daily accomplished the work given to her in the midst of her limitations. Mary's unfair and uncomfortable situation didn't hinder God from fulfilling his purpose for her life.

The promise is based on God's grace. The promise comes by faith. All of Abraham's children will certainly receive the promise. And it is not only for those who are ruled by the law. Those who have the same faith that Abraham had are also included. He is the father of us all.

—Romans 4:16 NIrV

As mysterious and severe as this truth is, consider this: the reality of "what is," not the fantasy of "what could be," is the place where God's will is accomplished in our lives. Learn to make peace with the mysteries of surrender, submission, endurance.

That day when I confessed to Donna, she told me to go home, and I did. The angel of the Lord told Hagar to go back to Sarai, and she did. God's blessing came inside the obedience.

All of these life truths played themselves out in the books I was writing during this season of life. The Sierra Jensen series was completed. I finished three books in the Christy and Todd: The College Years series, and all eight Glenbrooke books were in print. I had also written two more teen books, *Christy Miller's Diary* and *Departures*, and was just putting the finishing touches on a gift book titled *Tea at Glenbrooke*, when I ended up back in the hospital for another procedure. That was followed by another surgery the day after Christmas.

I was ready to go home and return to life as usual when my doctor came in, looked me in the eye, and said, "The growth we removed was malignant."

Life as I knew it was doused like a fire in a downpour. Now I had to decide if I could, once again, make peace with God's mysteries.

Chapter 6

A BANNER WORD

Godly people ... do not fear bad news; they confidently trust the L*ORD to care for them.*

— PSALM 112:2, 7 NLT

I rolled into the new year once again confined to bed. The old travel companions, Fear and Doubt, showed up right on schedule and tried to set up camp. This time I kicked them out. No Fear allowed. No Doubt allowed. Hope and Faith were the two friends I invited along on the journey to healing this time. Their comfort brought me rest. Their cheer brought me joy.

The surgeon expressed confidence that he had managed to remove all of the cancerous growth, and it hadn't spread into the rest of my colon. Early detection was the key in my situation, and I was grateful my doctor was so thorough and cautious. All I could do at that point was take it easy, heal up, and have tests and blood work in two months.

It's a freaky thing to hear the words *malignant* and *cancer* and then be told to go home and wait to see if it spreads. How do you spend those two months? Do you scramble to put everything in your life in order and read everything you can on chemotherapy? Or do you block it out of your mind and live as you were living before the surgery? I wavered between the two.

In an effort to be about life as usual, I kept my appointment with the Lord on January 2. Every January, for more than fifteen years, I had set aside a full day to sit by the fire with a pot of tea, a lit candle, my Bible, and my journal. On that day of fresh beginnings, I would read through my journal from the year before and make notes in the margins. I was always amazed that many of the things I worried about never came to be. I could see patterns in the prayers I had written throughout the year. Themes often repeated themselves, and the same verses appeared in the thoughts I had tried to express on paper. I could see patterns in my life there on the pages.

Something elemental and essential occurred when I didn't limit the crafting of sentences to a procession of letters, dots, and dashes on my computer screen. As a word lover, I always experienced a returning-to-my-roots sort of connection with words every time I wrote. When I created words with pen in hand, pen to paper, breath and movement—voilà!—thoughts became visible. My vulnerable heart would come out of hiding, and I was willing to be known.

That's why setting aside an entire day to return to those many words scribbled throughout the year became more than a tradition or ritual. It became an act of worship. It was, and still is, a *Selah* moment—the Hebrew word for "pause and ponder"—during which I found myself once again in awe of great God.

This tradition was birthed when I was going through my journal on a winter's morn, searching for a quote I had logged there the year before. I noticed that the same word appeared in my musings a number of times. I had just started a new journal, so I penned the recurring theme word from the previous year at the front and wrote, "Lord, did you do this? Did you repeat this word throughout my life last year? Do you have another word for me for this year?"

I returned to reading my Bible, praying, and journaling. As I did, a word floated into my thoughts. It was a single word, all by itself, appearing in my thoughts like a lone, white, puffy cloud in a deep blue sky. The word continued to float past the picture window of my mind. I wrote it down. I thought about it. I looked up verses related to that word. Cautiously I asked the Lord if that was the word for the year. If it was, then I wanted to receive it with open hands.

Throughout that year the banner word kept popping up. I shared it with my daughter and my closest friends. One of them said she had started asking God for a banner word several years ago, and he always gave her one. The word became "like a theme song," she said. "All year long I hear the melody running through my life."

The thought of God being that deliberate and that artistic as he directed my life was thrilling. Was this his way of expressing his love language to me? He created me to love words. Why would he not delight in giving me one specific word each year?

Every January since then I have sat before the Lord with open hands and my heart bowed before him. I tell him that if he should choose to once again be generous and give me another word, I will receive it with a grateful heart. I know that God doesn't have to do this for me. I know it could become twisted if I put too much emphasis on receiving a word each year or focus on the gift of the word itself instead of on the Giver of the word.

God has always given me a word during these times. They have turned into the sweetest, most intimate times with Jesus—our own after-Christmas gift exchange. He gives me a word, and I give him all the days and hours of the year ahead. I know they are already his allotted gift to me, but I give them back all the same. The best part is that I can never outgive God. Everything I give him, he gives back, pressed down and overflowing.

Sometimes the word of the year tumbles around in my thoughts before my January appointment with God. One year, on Thanksgiving

Day, it came to me as clear as if a bell were ringing. Another year I didn't have a clue what the word was going to be. But as I journaled a summary of the banner words that had been themes during the previous five years, the new word emerged. There was a pattern. Always a pattern. Like signposts along a trail that indicate how God is accomplishing his purposes.

My January appointment with the Lord after the cancer diagnosis was a difficult one. I thought I'd heard the word for the new year as it thundered through my spirit a few days before Christmas. It came upon me before the unexpected colon surgery, but I didn't write it down. It wasn't the word I wanted to hear.

On the first Saturday in January, still ignoring the word that had rolled in like thunder over Christmas, I eased my healing body into my snuggle chair and took a sip of tea. "Lord, I'm here," I whispered. "I'm listening. I'm yours."

The same word that had boomed in my ears before Christmas still clung to my spirit. It wasn't going away.

The word was *loss*.

What sort of loss would take place in the year ahead? Would we lose my dad? Would I lose my hair if a future diagnosis confirmed new malignancies? Would we lose our home? Would I lose my book contracts with the publisher that was now in the midst of an aggressive transformation? Or would I lose my life?

Any and all of the above were possible and even probable the way things were going. I really wanted a different word. I didn't want to be a victim of grace who lived with the word *loss* draped over my life for a year. My fingers flipped through the pages of my Bible until I came to the second chapter of Job and read his response to his wife when everything started to go so terribly wrong in his life without any explanation of what was happening or what he had done to deserve it. His wife wanted it all to be over. The losses of home, livestock, children, and health had come one right after the other. It was too much for anyone. I imagine she was beyond devastated when she told Job to "curse God and die!" (Job 2:9).

Job's response was, "Should we accept only good things from the hand of God and never anything bad?" (verse 10 NLT).

I wrote Job's words in my journal. Then I drew in a deep breath, opened my hands, and told the Lord I was willing to receive with gratitude the word he wanted to give me for the year. And indeed, that word was *loss*.

The first loss came a few weeks later when our son went off to film school two thousand miles away. Everything I had heard my friends report about the empty-nest syndrome became a reality in my little nest. I would wander into his bedroom in the middle of the day when no one was home and stretch out on his bed, burrowing my nose in his pillow just to catch a faint whiff of his lingering scent.

We had gone through almost all we had in savings to cover medical bills and the ongoing care of an ailing parent. At the same time we were working out the expenses of our children's education. We made some good decisions about what really mattered, and we made some bad decisions based on projections of what we hoped would happen.

The best loss of that year was the loss of the malignant growth. That was a good loss. An excellent loss. Two months after the surgery, I went in for tests, and my blood work was clear. No further procedures or treatments were required. I was free to go on with life as usual. Only nothing about that year felt usual.

Before summer began I lost the arrangement I had with the publisher I had worked with for a long time. The future of the Christy Miller and Sierra Jensen books appeared to be in jeopardy, as there were no plans to continue printing the series. I was losing the books and the publishing relationship, but saddest of all was the loss of these characters. I felt there were more stories to write about Christy, Todd, and the rest of the gang, but my signature was attached to the bottom line of some significant contracts that legally clarified what I could and couldn't do with these books.

On top of that loss, my stream of writing contracts dried up. No projects waited for me to complete. It felt odd after spending the past fifteen years always being on deadline, always being engaged in a running conversation in my head with imaginary characters. This loss put me in a wide-open place where I was available for God to do a new thing.

It seemed as if God was clearing the way for something new by taking away what was old and familiar. Have you noticed how that happens? When we are down to nothing, God is up to something.

Learning to Forgive From the Heart

With no projects of my own to work on, I was invited to join several other writers to explore some coauthored projects. One of the writers was well known, and the project we were discussing could turn into something big.

On the second day of our brainstorming meetings, one of the other writers said to me, "I noticed yesterday from some of the things you said that you are harboring unforgiveness in your heart."

His words startled me. I wasn't holding anything against anybody. At least I didn't think I was. Sure, I'd talked the day before about some of the unfair and unhappy things that had happened during the years I had been writing and my husband and I had been doing youth ministry together. But that was the past. We had moved on to other things, and I didn't want to look back.

See, I am doing a new thing!
Now it springs up;
do you not perceive it?
I am making a way in
the wilderness
and streams in the
wasteland.
—Isaiah 43:19

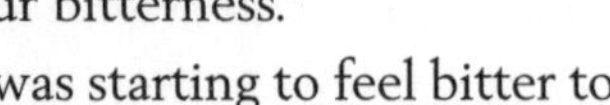

"But you need to look back," he said. "You need to identify the root of your bitterness."

I was starting to feel bitter toward this fellow author. I hardly knew him; yet here he was, poking at the scar tissue in my heart's most hidden and vulnerable corner. With a sense of panic, I looked at Melody, one of the other writers who was a long-time, trusted friend. She and I had been through a lot together. I expected her to affirm that I should shake off this evaluation of my heart.

Instead, Melody's expression indicated that she was in agreement with him. "It was the strangest thing," she said. "At four o'clock this morning, I suddenly woke up and felt an overwhelming need to pray for you. Don't freak out when I say this, but I had dreamed that you were being tortured."

My spirit went very still. I had been awake at exactly 4:00 a.m. too. But I wasn't up writing. This time I was lying flat in bed feeling as if all the air was being squeezed out of my lungs. My head pounded as if I was being chased, and I was running hard to get away. I had awakened from the terrible nightmare and chalked it all up to being stressed and worried about money, family, and health. I had been in this place of middle-of-the-night terror before but had never linked the sense of being tormented to my lack of forgiveness.

I told the group that I had been awake at the same time Melody had her dream, and I had indeed felt as if I were being tortured. The straightforward writer immediately said, "Ah! That's a good indicator of what's going on in your heart. You'll find that precise description in Matthew 18 for the servant who was unforgiving. The master had forgiven his entire debt, but then the servant tried to collect what others owed him. The master found out, and here's what happened."

He quoted the last part of Matthew 18 as if he, too, had once experienced this same sense of torment, and that's why he recognized the problem in me. "'Shouldn't you have had mercy on your fellow servant just as I had on you?' In anger his master handed him over to the jailers to be tortured, until he should pay back all he owed. This is how my heavenly Father will treat each of you unless you forgive your brother or sister from your heart" (verses 33–35).

It's hard to explain why this fellow writer's words didn't offend me. His expression was so sincere and his tone so free of any condemnation that it made me thirsty to hear what he was going to say next. He clearly knew what he was talking about. He cared about me and was trying to help me.

"The key is to forgive from your heart, not just your head. Forgiving is not just letting go of some injustice or assault and hoping that the passing of time will cover it up." His eyes were clear and piercing, yet filled with compassion. "We must name the sin that was done to us and choose, from the heart, to no longer hold on to it."

He asked if I wanted to be rid of the list of hurts and injustices I was keeping. I'm sure it was the Holy Spirit who in that moment softened my spirit and prompted me to say, "Yes, I do. I want to forgive from my heart and be free from old hurts and pains."

The writer asked if I wanted him to help me as I prayed. I nodded.

"Begin your prayer by saying, 'From my heart I choose to forgive.' Then name the people and the hurts you are releasing them from."

I bowed my head, and with Melody beside me, her hand on my shoulder for support, I prayed, "Father, from my heart I choose to forgive the church that treated my husband and me unfairly."

"Wait. Stop."

I looked up. No one had ever stopped me midprayer before.

"You're not praying from your heart," he said.

"Excuse me? Yes, I am. I mean this. I really do."

"No, you don't. You see, it's not the entire church that wounded you. Who was the person who sinned against you and your husband?"

The name was instantly on my lips. The face loomed in my thoughts.

"You see that person, don't you?"

I nodded. Something deep inside of me ached. The hurt was still fresh. It hadn't diminished after all these years, even though I had thought it had.

"What did that person do? In a word. Identify it. What was the sin that person committed?"

I knew what the offense was even though I don't think I'd ever identified it before. The word that permeated my thoughts was *betrayal.* That was the sin—one that Jesus knew well.

"Let's try again," he suggested.

I bowed my head, closed my eyes. I could still see the betrayer's face, and I went through the mental list of all the unfair things that person had said and done. I couldn't pray. I was furious all over again, all these years later.

My patient writer-friend said, "This is really deep for you, isn't it?"

I looked up and nodded.

"Do you want to forgive him?"

"Yes."

"Why?"

"I want to release him so that I can be free as well. What he did wasn't right, but I think that, in a way, he didn't know what he was doing at the time. He didn't realize the impact his actions would have." As soon as I articulated those thoughts, a Scripture passage came to mind. As Jesus hung on the cross, betrayed and unjustly accused, he prayed, "Father, forgive them, for they do not know what they are doing" (Luke 23:34).

If I regard iniquity in my heart, the Lord will not hear me.

—Psalm 66:18 KJV

I also thought of all I had been forgiven of when I surrendered my life to Christ. I asked God one time, and he wiped out all my sin as if it had never happened. Yet for years I had harbored unforgiveness. I held on to the list of infractions against several people as if it were ammunition I could pull out and one day use against them if the need arose. It's not safe to store explosives in your heart. One spark, and everything can be blown to smithereens.

Now that I could see where I was wrong and why I needed to forgive, I bowed my head and began the prayer again. This time as I quietly spoke the words from my heart, a reservoir of tears broke free, and

I cried as I had never cried before. The tears flowed from the corners of my eyes, but no sounds accompanied them. These were tears from the wellspring of my soul.

"Ah, there it is," my writer-friend said with deep understanding. "You're there now. You're at the heart level. Now it means something when you say 'from my heart.' Go ahead, tell the Lord what's on your heart."

I began by asking God to forgive me for holding on to the bitterness and unforgiveness toward this particular person. He was one of God's children. Using the words "from my heart I choose to forgive," I stated his first name and the sin. As soon as the words tumbled off my lips, I felt a lightness return to my spirit—a sense of serenity I hadn't realized had been absent.

Looking up, I said, "There's someone else I need to forgive." The tears kept coming in a silent stream. I named the person's first name, identified the exact hurt, and realized that in human eyes I had a right to continue to hold the infraction against this person. What they had done wounded me deeply. I had tried to forgive and forget. But if I allowed myself to replay the infraction in my mind I always felt a sense of injustice rising and I knew that by human standards I had the right to seek revenge.

But now, when I saw this person's face before me and remembered vividly the violation, I went deep into my heart rather than my head. From my heart I chose to forgive, to release this person.

Neither Melody nor our writer-friend who stood beside me as I prayed knew what the offense was, nor did I need to state any details. All I did was name the roots of the offense, and surprisingly the first root of sin that came to mind was betrayal once again. This was a person I had trusted, someone who should have been a safe place for me. So what this person did had rocked my world. I had shared the infraction with only a handful of people who told me that I couldn't possibly understand what they had gone through. It gave me power to be able to say, "Oh yes, I do understand." Details were not needed and for everyone else the story went untold.

Years earlier I had parceled out a pardon for the person who hurt me, but that limited clemency had largely come from my human reservoir of mercy, not from God's unending ocean of grace. I had managed to embrace the infraction all these years with enough measured control so that if I ever wanted to slip into the role of victim, I could do so. I had kept the memory of the traumatic event alive and ready to call into play if I ever needed sympathy.

As I stood in the middle of my two trusted writer-friends and prayed, from my heart, to completely forgive this person, chains were being broken in the spiritual realm. I was releasing that person, and in that same instant, I was being released.

> [To forgive is to] set a prisoner free [and] discover that the prisoner was yourself.
> —*Lewis Smedes, Forgive and Forget*

In that moment I transferred the responsibility for forgiving that person to God. Instead of trying to muster up enough mercy not to hold the offense against the person who sinned against me, I was letting go, turning to my faithful heavenly Father, and placing the burden and responsibility on him. "Father, you forgive them. They don't know what they're doing."

The heavy lifting of forgiving wasn't up to me. Instead, I entrusted it to my heavenly Father. He rolled away the stone in my heart. He brought back to life that which was dead inside of me.

A Kindred Victim of Grace

What happened to me on that day of praying with my writing friends was life giving. The experience of forgiveness reminded me of John 11. Lazarus was sick. Very sick. His sisters, Mary and Martha, sent for Jesus. The big mystery in this story on first read is that Jesus didn't answer their call right away. We know what that's like when we pray and nothing happens.

In this story we read that "Jesus loved Martha and her sister and Lazarus. So when he heard that Lazarus was sick, he stayed where he was two more days" (verses 5–6).

Jesus loved them. He knew what was happening. He knew they were in a terrible situation and that human efforts wouldn't make a difference. And yet he didn't come. He didn't respond immediately to Mary and Martha's frantic request.

No one can control Christ. None of us can manipulate his decisions based on our needs or demand that he do what we think is best. Jesus moves as his Father directs, not as humans dictate. He told his disciples that Lazarus had "fallen asleep," but that he was going to "wake him up" (verse 11 NLT).

The words Jesus used confused his disciples. In their human understanding, they surmised that since Lazarus was sleeping, he must have been getting better. But Lazarus wasn't getting better. He died. Mary and Martha prepared his body for burial in the traditional way by wrapping it in strips of linen that had been soaked in fragrant oils. Friends and family gathered for the traditional thirty-day mourning period—three days of very heavy mourning followed by four days of heavy mourning, and then lighter mourning for the remainder of the month.

During this time of great loss, pain, and sorrow, Jesus made the thirty-mile journey on foot to Bethany. Lazarus had been in the tomb for four days. This number of days was significant, because the Jews believed that the spirit hovered over the body for three days before departing this earth and entering the hereafter. Jesus didn't arrive during that period of lingering but rather after all who were present and mourning had gone from very heavy mourning to heavy mourning. All hope was gone. Lazarus had departed. And Jesus hadn't come when he was summoned.

When Martha heard that Jesus was on his way, she went out to meet him. Her sister, Mary, stayed home. This was the same Mary who had sat at Jesus' feet when he had been in their home on an earlier occasion. Mary had soaked in all of Christ's teaching while her sister, Martha, had bustled about to prepare food, beds, and beverages for Jesus and his followers. We're familiar with the story of that dinner at their home in Bethany, because when Martha complained to Jesus that Mary wasn't helping with all the work around the house, Jesus told Martha that she was "worried and upset about many things," but only one thing was needed. Her sister, Mary, had chosen what was better, and Jesus said, "It will not be taken away from her" (Luke 10:41, 42).

Even with such an affirmation of what was needed—full-hearted attentiveness to the Lord—Mary wasn't the one who ran to Jesus. Martha was. She didn't wait for Jesus to arrive at their house. She went to him. Grace gives us the confidence to go boldly before the Lord at all times, but especially during our times of need.

Let us then approach God's throne of grace with confidence, so that we may receive mercy and find grace to help us in our time of need.

—Hebrews 4:16

The first thing Martha said to Jesus was, "Lord, if you had been here, my brother would not have died" (John 11:21).

Haven't we all thought the same thing over the years in a number of horrible and painful situations? We pray when things start to look bad and wait for the Lord to answer, but he's silent. When the worst happens, at least the worst in our way of viewing life, then we're prone to say to the Lord, "If you had been here, this wouldn't have happened. Where were you? Why didn't you act on this earlier? You could have changed this or stopped this in the beginning."

Martha did a better job than most of us when it came to moving from discouragement to faith. After she said openly and honestly to the Lord, "If you had been here, my brother would not have died," she added, "but I know that even now God will give you whatever you ask" (verses 21–22).

Wow, Martha, such faith! "Even now God will give you whatever you ask." She didn't stay stuck on the tragedy of Lazarus's death. She didn't get stuck on the blame game that has been with us since Eden and continues to play into our psyches every time something goes the way we don't want it to go. Whose fault was it that Lazarus died? Was it Jesus' fault because he didn't answer her cry when it came to his ears?

Martha let go of the blaming and finger pointing. With that simple bridge word *but,* she moved from the past into the present with great faith and said, "Even now ..." We have been given the same empowering grace that infused Martha with the confidence and boldness to stand before her Savior. Jesus calls us his friends and loves us the same way he loved Martha, her sister, and Lazarus. Grace always gives us the freedom to say what we really think and feel. This beautiful path always leads us to life.

A much greater purpose will be accomplished in the kingdom of God when we relinquish our objectives, our sorrows, our demands for justice. "Even now" God is pouring out his grace so we can see once again that, yes, we are victims—victims of grace.

What happened next between Martha and Jesus was a tender exchange. He told her what would happen. With straightforward words Jesus said, "Your brother will rise again" (verse 23).

How often we say things like, "I just wish the Lord would tell me what's going on" or "If I knew what God was doing in all this, I would be able to trust him more." Once again, it seems the blessing happens inside the obedience, not when we stand to the side, arms folded, demanding that God let us in on his secrets.

Jesus let Martha in on his secret this time. He told her what was going to happen, but she had no context for the truth. People don't come back to life after being in a tomb for four days. Even so, she expressed trust in the Lord when she said that she knew her brother would rise again in the resurrection at the end of all things.

To this declaration of faith, Jesus responded with an even bigger secret. He revealed to Martha one of his "I AM" titles. God first used this title when he changed Abram's name to Abraham. On that day God affirmed his covenant promise that Abraham would become the father of a great nation and declared, "I am God Almighty" (Genesis 17:1).

When God called to Moses from the midst of the burning bush and told him to go to Egypt to deliver God's children from bondage, Moses asked whom he should say sent him to deliver them. God's reply was, "I AM WHO I AM" (Exodus 3:14).

At the end of all things, at the final resurrection Martha referred to, God will declare, "I am the Alpha and the Omega, the First and the Last, the Beginning and the End" (Revelation 22:13).

During the three years of Christ's ministry on earth, he continually gave his disciples pieces of this great I AM title. He used visual aids when he told them, "I am the bread of life" (John 6:35); "I am the true vine" (John 15:1); "I am the light of the world" (John 8:12); "I am the good shepherd" (John 10:11); "I am the way and the truth and the life" (John 14:6); and "I am the gate" (John 10:9).

Face-to-face with Martha, Jesus declared perhaps the most powerful of all his "I AM" statements: "I am the resurrection and the life" (John 11:25).

Christ graciously gave her that truth along with the explanation, "The one who believes in me will live, even though they die; and whoever lives by believing in me will never die." The way of salvation was all there in a single sentence. Then Jesus asked her, "Do you believe this?" (verses 25–26).

Martha said yes.

For all of us, the essential foundation for everything lies in this profound declaration of our Lord. He is "the resurrection and the life." We are invited to believe in him. When we leave these bodies of ours, as we all will one day, we enter into eternal life with the great I AM. In light of that grand view and greater picture, our deep hurts and painful wounds are only temporary. One day we will be healed. We will have new bodies when we go to be with the Lord, and he will wipe away every tear.

Our inability to forgive robs us of living freely during the limited days that are given us. More than that, the accounts we hold against others can bind them and keep them from living fully the lives God has planned for them. A hint of this truth is seen at the end of Lazarus's story.

Jesus asked Mary and Martha to show him where Lazarus had been laid. He saw Mary weeping along with the others who followed him to the tomb, still in heavy mourning. Jesus was "deeply moved in spirit and troubled," and then "Jesus wept" (verses 33, 35).

When the Jews saw Jesus weeping, they said, "See how he loved him!" (verse 36).

I wonder. Was Jesus weeping for Lazarus, or for those at the tomb who were in such distress? Or was he weeping for all those he knows by heart who refuse to bow before him? Unlike Martha, they have said to him, "No, I don't believe you are the Christ. I don't believe you are the resurrection and the life." Because of their unbelief, they won't enter into eternal life with Christ. Could this have been the deeper reason for Jesus' tears?

Jesus went to Lazarus's tomb and again was deeply moved. He gave the command to roll the stone away from the opening. He could have moved the stone himself, but he wanted the women to give their permission.

Martha protested, saying there would be a fetid odor of rotting flesh, since Lazarus's body had been in the tomb for four days. His answer to her was personal. "Did I not tell you that if you believe, you will see the glory of God?" (verse 40).

I saw this pattern played out as my two writer-friends prayed with me. It was as if Jesus was asking me to open up the tombs in which I had placed relationships that were dead to me. I had wrapped up the carcasses with strips of accusations and their own acts of injustice and locked them away where the life was gone but the remains were rotting. I didn't want to open up those tombs. I didn't want to do the hard work of rolling away the stones I had placed in front of those tombs in my heart.

Yet it was as if Jesus was asking me if I believed. Did I believe that he was the resurrection and the life? Did I believe that he could bring life to what was dead? Did I believe that if I obeyed him, I would see God's glory?

Mary and Martha obeyed. They did their part by allowing the stone to be moved away. Then they stood back, and Jesus took it from there. He prayed, beginning with words of thanks to his Father. Then the miracle happened—the miracle that had been in motion from the moment the women sent word to Jesus.

The familiar part of this story was about to happen. Rembrandt painted this dramatic moment. For centuries children's Bible storybooks have included this miracle. It is both wonderful and terrifying to us.

The moment you began praying, a command was given. And now I am here to tell you what it was, for you are very precious to God.

—Daniel 9:23 NLT

Jesus stood before the open tomb and called out in a loud voice, "Lazarus, come out!" (verse 43). And Lazarus came out! He was still bound in strips of linen, and a cloth was wrapped around his face. He was just as Mary and Martha had left him before the stone had been rolled across the cave's opening. Now the tomb had been opened, and Jesus had performed the miracle. He made one who was dead to them come back to life.

The women had one more step to take in this process of resurrection. Jesus told them to "loose him … and let him go" (verse 44 KJV).

A live person was inside the mummylike encasement, and he needed to be set free. New life was waiting to be released, and the sisters were the ones assigned to unwrap and release their brother from the grave clothes.

What I found most interesting about Jesus' directive was the choice of words. Jesus told them to "loose," "release," "untie" Lazarus. The Greek word here literally means to "break, dissolve, destroy, melt, pull off."

Depending on what Mary and Martha used as the embalming oil to moisten the strips of linen as they wrapped their brother's body, the encasement may have dried like a cast. If so, releasing him would have required the use of water, and they would have had to get their hands in there, digging with their fingernails through the layers.

I see this sort of important work being done by the clients my husband counsels. As a counselor, he leads them to an understanding that forgiveness is essential if they are ever going to be free. That process of forgiveness can sometimes require more than just moving away the stone from their hearts and the willingness to open up a topic once again. It can involve this same sort of verbal hands-on pulling away of layers and working hard to release the many strips of just and true accusations to get to the human that God so dearly longs to set free.

Jesus told the women to do two things: "loose him" and "let him go." The Greek word for "let him go" is *aphiemi*, which means to "send forth, lay aside, leave, let go, omit, forgive."

Forgive.

This is why Lazarus's story spoke so personally to me as I went through the process of forgiving those who had betrayed and deeply wounded me. Jesus asks each of us, as he asked Martha, "Do you believe?" And if we do, then we will obey him. When he says to open up a topic or a relationship we have bound up so tightly and buried with mourning, then we will do as he says and move the stone. He is the resurrection and the life. He is the one who calls back to life those who were dead to us and those who were dead spiritually, separated from him and the eternal life he planned for them from the beginning.

This picture of forgiveness came full circle when I dug deeper to find out more about the Greek word *aphiemi*. It's used only one other time in the New Testament. Can you guess where?

In Luke 23:34 Jesus said, "Father, *aphiemi* them, for they do not know what they are doing." Forgive. Release. Untie. Let go. This is an excellent loss. A loss of anxiety, a loss of tormentors in the night, the loss of a toxic heaviness that seeps into our souls and can poison all our conversations, relationships, and thoughts.

Loss was a good word for me that year. I was graced by Father God many times over that year through the losses I experienced. By "graced" I mean that every time I needed clarity and strength, his grace empowered me so that I could go to him as Martha did and converse with him openly and honestly. And then he provided the grace to do what he commanded me to do.

Before the year ended, one more painful and significant loss came. My father left this earth and went to heaven on a crisp October morning. After five and a half years of being a prisoner in his own body, he was set free, but before he left this earth, he did some untying and letting go of his own.

Chapter 7

THE DAY MY DADDY WINKED AT ME

Behold, how good and pleasant it is
when brothers dwell in unity!

—Psalm 133:1 ESV

On the tragic morning of September 11, 2001, I was at my parents' home in Southern California, helping my mom as she cared for my dad. More than five years after the paralyzing stroke had robbed him of the gift of words, he had declined to the point where we called in hospice.

The morning that the twin towers crumbled, I was packing my bags for an eleven o'clock flight out of Los Angeles back home to Portland. My brother-in-law called and told us to turn on the television. We did, and all packing stopped. Like hundreds of thousands of other travelers, I didn't go anywhere that day.

We kept the TV off in the room where my father lay in his hospital bed. When the hospice nurse arrived that afternoon, we spoke in lowered voices in the other room.

"He shouldn't still be here," the nurse said. "His kidneys are barely functioning. His pulse is low and faint. He is hanging on for a reason. I often see patients who linger like this because they have someone in their life they need to make peace with. Can you think of anyone he has an unresolved relationship with?"

I have cared for you since
you were born.
Yes, I carried you before
you were born.
I will be your God throughout
your lifetime—
until your hair is white with age.
I made you, and I will
care for you.
I will carry you along
and save you.
—Isaiah 46:3–4 NLT

My mom and I looked at each other, unsure of who that might be.

I slipped into my dad's room and saw that his eyes were open for the first time since I had arrived four days earlier. Did he sense something was going on from hearing the sounds of the television in the other room or our whispers with the hospice nurse?

Going to my dad's bedside and stroking his snowy white hair, I noticed the tight worry lines that ran across his forehead. He had looked that way for days, as if he was in pain, but the hospice nurse assured us he was receiving everything he needed not to experience any discomfort.

For some reason, as I looked at my dad, I remembered a time in junior high when I was experiencing great discomfort from the orthodontic treatment I was going through. My mouth had endured tooth extractions, braces positioned and tightened, and rubber bands that snapped in my mouth at unwanted moments. The worst phase of treatments involved headgear—one of those archaic torture devices with a neck strap and wires that torqued me to tears.

During those three years of procedures to straighten my "cattywampus teeth," as my dad called them, he would drive me to and from my orthodontist appointments. On one of those numerous expensive trips, I was crying and telling my dad that I didn't care if my jaw didn't line up and my teeth were cattywampus. It hurt too much, and I wanted to stop.

He firmly told me to stop crying. This was for my good, and I'd have to learn to live with the pain.

I stopped crying. Inwardly I remember feeling angry at him. He didn't understand how hard this was to endure. He didn't know how tired I was of all the visits, all the hours of leaning back in that salmon-pink dental chair, being stuck in that reclined position and having pieces of metal fit over my teeth.

The anger eventually subsided. In time the braces and the headgear did their work. Then one grand and glorious day during my high-school sophomore year, all the pieces of orthodontia were removed, and my perfectly straightened teeth were cleaned and polished. I rinsed and spit and was handed a mirror. The reflection that smiled back at me with big white teeth looked very different from any likeness I'd ever seen in the mirror before. I'd been transformed.

Now, all these years later, as my dad lay unresponsive in his bed, I gave him a big smile. It was a thank-you smile for all the years he had worked an extra job on weeknights selling tools in the Sears department store in downtown Santa Ana just so I could have straight teeth and a bite that matched up. I knew then that I would have been a different person if I hadn't had my teeth straightened. I would have gone through life smiling a lot less. I would have had much less confidence.

Dad was right. All the pain had been worth it. I knew that for him, all the pain, frustration, and discomfort he had gone through for more than five years with his cattywampus legs would soon be over. He had trusted Christ as his Savior. He believed Jesus' words to Martha when he told her he was the resurrection and the life. My father would soon be catching a reflection of his new resurrected body in the shining gold streets of heaven.

I gave his hand a squeeze and smiled again at the thought of what awaited him in glory.

His solemn blue eyes met mine. I was surprised that in his diminished state, he was focusing on me.

"Hi, Daddy," I said softly.

His left eyebrow rose slightly. I leaned closer. I hadn't managed this much of a connection with him during this entire visit or the visit two months before.

"You've fought a good fight, Dad. You've run a good race. You can go, you know. You can go to heaven. We'll see you there."

He let out a sigh. I thought it was a sigh. His breath was so diminished, it was more like a long exhale. His lower lip drooped and quivered as if he had a tic.

Remembering what the hospice nurse had said earlier, I asked, "Dad, is there anyone you would like me to call for you? Anyone you want to say good-bye to or maybe make peace with?"

A long, more breathy "Yaaaa" escaped ever so slightly from his worn-out lungs.

My heart pounded. He was very present and connected to me.

"Okay, who is it? Who do you want to make peace with?" I went down the list of all the people in our immediate family and moved on to other friends and relatives. He gave no indication that he wanted to connect with any of them.

Then I remembered his brother, Uncle Harry. It had been many years since I had seen or heard about Uncle Harry. The two brothers had their share of disagreements over the years, and it had been a long time since they had had any communication with each other.

"Daddy, do you want me to call Uncle Harry for you?"

His lips trembled at the name of his only living brother, and tears spilled down his face. "Yaaa" was his breathy reply.

"Okay, I'm going to call Uncle Harry, and I'm going to tell him that you love him."

"Yaaa."

"And I'm going to tell him that you forgive him, and you want him to forgive you."

I had no idea what these two brothers had to apologize to each other about, but it seemed this was the direction my dad wanted me to go because he pressed my hand weakly and issued another faint "Yaaa."

I went to the phone in the kitchen, flipped through my parents' Rolodex, and found the number. I dialed it while my mom and the hospice nurse were still talking in the living room and was disappointed when the answering machine picked up my call. I left a message, asking Uncle Harry to call me back.

Two minutes later the phone rang. It was Uncle Harry.

"Uncle Harry?" I began. "This is your niece, Robin."

"Who?" he said.

I repeated my name and explained to Uncle Harry how weak my dad had become and that hospice was helping us care for him. Then I took the phone into my dad's room. My father's eyes followed me, his left eyebrow lifted again ever so slightly, the way it always did when he was trying to ask a question.

I took the phone over to him and held it just a few inches away from his ear. "This is your brother. It's Harry. He's on the phone."

Tears cascaded down my father's face. Silent tears from the wellspring of his soul.

"Uncle Harry? My dad wants me to tell you that he loves you."

A deep guttural sound of choked agreement gathered in my dad's throat. I kept going. "My dad wants you to also know that he forgives you, and he wants you to forgive him. He wants there to be peace on both sides."

I listened closely for Uncle Harry's response. The phone line was silent.

"Hello? Uncle Harry? Are you still there?"

It was another moment before he said, "You have no idea what you've done, girl. Put the phone to his ear. I have something to say to him now."

I couldn't tell if Uncle Harry was about to give my dad a blessing or a curse, but I put the phone to my dad's ear. I wasn't able to hear what Uncle Harry said, but I could tell by the full flow of tears from my dad's eyes, accompanied by the choked and weak sounds that welled up from his gut and came out through his uncooperative lips, that this was what he wanted. This was what he had held on for. He was making peace with his brother.

As I took the phone away from my dad's ear, his eyes rolled back from exhaustion. "Uncle Harry? It's me again. It's Robin."

"You have no idea what you've done," he said again. Then he added, "We should have said these things to each other many years ago. Thank you for making the call."

Uncle Harry was choked up as he asked me to be the one to call him when the time came and my dad passed away. Harry said his health wouldn't allow him to fly cross-country for the memorial service, but he wanted to know when it was. I promised I would call him, and then I said good-bye to the uncle I had only seen half a dozen times in my life.

When I looked at my dad, the tears had already begun to dry on his cheeks. His eyes were closed. And best of all, the worry lines were gone. His forehead was smooth, and his expression was as peaceful as a sleeping child. Even the air in the room seemed fresher.

Mom and the hospice nurse made their way back into the room and found me standing beside the bed with the phone in one hand and my dad's hand in the other. Tears streamed from the corner of my eyes, but I couldn't stop smiling.

"What are you doing?" my mom asked.

"I just called Uncle Harry."

"You did?"

I nodded.

"Did your father have a chance to hear his voice?" The hospice nurse reached over to check his pulse.

"Yes, he did." I went on to tell them the whole event that had transpired over the past five minutes. They looked at me and at each other and then back at my dad.

"It's very good that you made the call," the nurse said. "He was waiting for that final connection." She bent her head over the chart and made notes.

My mom started her familiar routine of checking each of the tubes connected to different parts of dad's body. As she worked, she scolded me politely in front of the nurse. "How do you know that's what your father wanted? He hasn't tried to communicate with anyone in weeks. Months."

She wasn't turned toward Dad's face. But I was.

He opened both eyes and looked directly at me. Once again his sudden gaze startled me. I had spent my life looking into those baby blues of his, listening to his puns, trying to match his quick wit, and always hoping to receive one of his trademark winks. His winks meant, "You got that pun, didn't you? No one else caught it, but you did. You're my girl. That's why. You just stepped into the secret. We share this, just you and me."

With my gaze fixed on my dad, I answered my mom's remarks with confidence. "This was what dad wanted. That's why I called Uncle Harry."

At that moment, with a single, effortless motion, my daddy winked at me. He winked! And then he closed his eyes again.

My mom and the hospice nurse looked up from their tasks. Both of them were too slow to see the wink.

"It won't be long now," the hospice nurse said.

I choked back the tears and left the room. No one else had seen what I had seen. No one else had heard what I had heard. Returning the phone to the cradle in the kitchen, I glanced at the TV that was playing the news without sound. Images of smoke billowing from the wreckage of the twin towers took my breath away. Bewildered firefighters slumped on the streets of New York City, covered in soot.

The God of all grace, who called you to his eternal glory in Christ, after you have suffered a little while, will himself restore you and make you strong, firm and steadfast.

—1 Peter 5:10

I went outside to get some air. I remembered the way Hannah had wept openly before the Lord in the temple. She cried so hard and with such passion that Eli the priest thought she was drunk. My tears seemed to match hers in intensity as they came from a deep and troubled place. The world was in chaos. My husband and daughter were hundreds of miles away in Portland. My son was more than two thousand miles away in Florida. My father was inching his way to heaven one shallow breath after another. And yet in the midst of all this anguish, he and his brother had just made peace.

Reconciliation comes into the rubble of many fallen lives and shines brightly like a single candle dispelling much darkness. And in the light of that candle, my daddy winked at me.

In all the terror, pain, and wickedness on this damaged planet, God's undaunted plan of reconciliation is ever alive. He wants us to get that, to step into the secret because we belong to him. In the wink of an eye, God's goodness and his unending love can prevail. What once was shattered can be redeemed.

On the day my father made peace with his brother, he closed his eyes, and for the next five weeks, he remained closed up and silent, breathing only in faint whispers. He never opened his eyes again. My mother was beside him when his last sigh was released, and no breath of earthly air was drawn back in.

We assembled at his bedside and timidly, reverently expressed an unexpected sense of lightness at his passing. He had been set free. He no longer inhabited the frame of flesh. His home was no longer in this world.

I could picture my dad running to Jesus, down the streets of gold, on legs that now cooperated. I could imagine him singing to his Savior the way he used to sing in the shower when his great tenor voice would reverberate throughout the house.

I saw in his final weeks how grace had opened the way to peace. All the years of disconnection from his brother were resolved in a single phone call. A call that was made long after my dad had the ability to use his own words to express what was on his heart. Being reconciled to his brother happened when grace made a way for forgiveness to be extended and expressed. The result was peace. Peace between two brothers, both victims of grace.

A Kindred Victim of Grace

Rachel and Leah were sisters in need of peace. They had their stretches of connection and disconnection, as well as their season of competition. It all started with a boy.

Not just any boy. This handsome stranger who arrived at the community well on a sunny afternoon was Jacob, the son of Isaac and grandson of Abraham. In the same way that Abraham had sent the servant back to his family's homeland when seeking a wife for Isaac, Isaac had in turn sent his son Jacob to the same region in search of a bride for himself.

No doubt Jacob had heard the story many times while he was growing up of how his parents met: how the servant had spotted Rebekah at the well, how she had watered all his camels, and how beautiful and strong she was. Now it was Jacob's turn to make the journey of more than five hundred miles to see if a beautiful woman might be waiting at a well for him.

Jacob—and not the servant this time—arrived at the well and did the waiting. All the other herdsmen from the area were there, waiting for the last shepherdess from the region to arrive so they could move the stone from the top of the cistern and water the flocks at the same time. As they were hanging out, Jacob asked if any of them knew his uncle Laban or any of his relatives.

"Here comes one of his daughters now," they answered.

And there she was. Rachel. The shepherdess they had all been waiting for. The woman Jacob had been hoping for. She "had a lovely figure and was beautiful" (Genesis 29:17). In his exuberance, Jacob moved the stone from the well by himself, and just as his mother had watered the servant's camels, Jacob repeated the generous gesture and watered all of Rachel's sheep.

Then the dashing hero did a dashing thing. He kissed Rachel! Right away Jacob told startled Rachel who he was and when he did, he began to weep.

What did poor, stunned Rachel do? She ran home to tell her father, Laban, who rushed out to meet Jacob. Laban embraced him, kissed him, and welcomed him into his home, declaring, "You are my own flesh and blood" (verse 14).

For a month Jacob pitched in with the work, just like one of the family. Laban decided that Jacob shouldn't continue to work for nothing, so he said to Jacob, "Tell me what your wages should be" (verse 15).

Jacob was ready with his answer. He wanted to marry Rachel. Can you imagine how many times their gazes had met over that first month Jacob was in Laban's household? How many times had the two of them closed their eyes and remembered what it felt like when Jacob impulsively kissed Rachel at the well that first day?

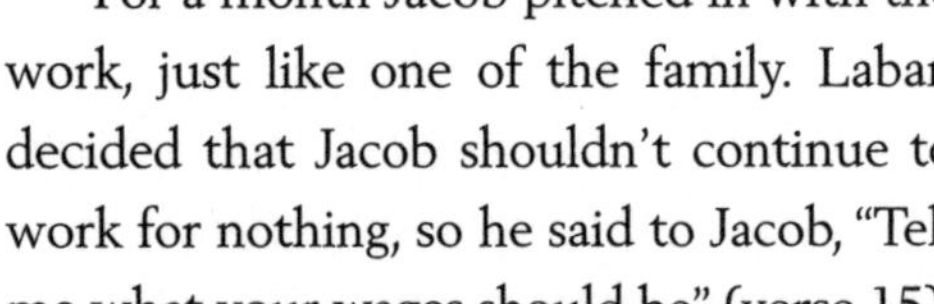

Grace and peace to you from God our Father and the Lord Jesus Christ.

—Ephesians 1:2

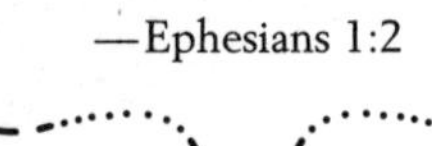

Laban and Jacob agreed that Jacob, who had arrived with nothing to offer for a bride, would work seven years to earn the right to marry Rachel. During those seven years, Jacob never wavered in his abiding passion for her. Those seven years "seemed like only a few days to him because of his love for her" (verse 20).

At last their wedding day came. The bride was thoroughly veiled, as was the tradition, and brought to Jacob so the long-awaited ceremony could take place. The vows were exchanged, and Jacob took his new bride to the prepared tent where he at last could fully express his passionate love for her.

In the morning, when the sun came up and filtered light illuminated the tent, Jacob awoke. He reached over to the woman beside him. For seven years he must have dreamed of this moment. Jacob turned to gaze upon the beautiful face of his beloved Rachel and … *Ack*! "Behold, it was Leah"! (verse 25 KJV).

I've often thought those were the saddest words in all the love stories recorded in the Bible. Laban had tricked Jacob after seven years of labor into taking as his wife Laban's eldest daughter. Poor Jacob! Poor Rachel! And most of all, poor Leah!

How could such a rift between two sisters ever be mended?

Jacob demanded that Laban keep his word and give Rachel to him as his wife. Laban agreed to hand Rachel over as a second wife, which was culturally acceptable at the time. There was, however, one condition. Jacob must promise to labor another seven years.

The two men agreed, and Rachel was given to Jacob that day in what must have been a tearful wedding. There they were, Jacob, Rachel, and Leah, all together for seven more years under Laban's thumb.

I must point out that Jacob wasn't completely innocent when it came to swindling a family member. The search for a wife was only part of the reason Jacob had sought his father's permission to journey to the land between the Tigris and Euphrates Rivers. Jacob was also, more importantly, in search of a new life because he had cheated his twin brother, Esau, out of both his birthright and their father's blessing, which belonged to the firstborn. Enraged Esau had plotted to kill Jacob. He was just waiting until after their father passed away to carry out his plan.

Jacob, whose name meant "heel-grabber," had fled his homeland, and now he knew the bitterness that came from deceit. He had been tricked into taking a bride he didn't want as well as working another seven years for the bride he did want. Jacob accepted this as his fate.

Stories like this make it clear that all the people in God's Book were real people. All of them were deeply marred in the fall, just as we were. All of us need a Savior. We bungle our most precious and valuable relationships, and yet God still pours out on us grace upon grace. Mercy upon mercy. We can be assured that God's intention in discipline is not to "get" us back, but always to get "us" back.

Just as my father reconciled with his brother at the end of his life, amazingly, Jacob and Esau had their moment of confrontation and restoration. A stunningly simple passage closes the story: "Isaac lived a hundred and eighty years. Then he breathed his last and died and was gathered to his people, old and full of years. And his sons Esau and Jacob buried him" (Genesis 35:28–29).

The two brothers came together to bury their father. Twins. Opponents for most of their lives. All the unfair dealings over the years were set aside. Siblings were reconciled.

How did the competition go between siblings Rachel and Leah? The two sisters had been given in marriage to the same man, and now they were in a race to have babies. Providing Jacob with heirs would prove each wife's worth and value to her husband, as well as establish her place in this triangle of a marriage.

We know that Jacob dearly loved Rachel. Her name meant "little lamb." Leah's name meant "cow." Poor Leah!

But you know what? God took tender care of his little cow. In Genesis 29:31, we read that "when the LORD saw that Leah was not loved, he enabled her to conceive, but Rachel remained childless."

Leah's first child was a boy. She named him Reuben, which has two connotations. First, the word sounds like the Hebrew phrase for "He has seen my misery." Leah knew that the Lord God was watching out for her. God had seen her misery. Second, the name Reuben literally means "See, a son." Any time others, including Rachel, called to this child or spoke his name, they would be repeating Leah's boast. Leah was the first of the two wives to have a baby—and look! It's a son. Say his name again, Rachel. See, a son!

As if that weren't demoralizing enough for Rachel, she remained barren while Leah conceived again and had another baby boy. She named this second son Simeon, which means "One who hears." Then she added this explanation: "Because the LORD heard that I am not loved" (verse 33).

What a deep valley of sorrow Leah must have wandered in because of her rivalry with her sister. What an emptiness she must have felt every day, knowing she wasn't loved. The Lord had opened her womb and blessed her with two sons, and yet the bitterness in her heart spilled over into the names she chose for them.

Leah became pregnant a third time and had another boy. The score was now Leah, three; Rachel, zip. We can only imagine the intensity of Rachel's jealousy and the soul wounds both sisters carried. I feel sorry for Jacob as well. Many evenings he probably wished he could have stayed out in the fields with the flocks instead of returning to camp. At home he had to deal with his wives' competition as well as his own shame and slow-brewing anger toward his father-in-law for putting all of them in this situation.

This wasn't what any of them had wanted.

It certainly wasn't the dreamy fairy tale we were ready for after the opening scene of this story. Boy meets girl, boy kisses girl, boy works for seven years to get girl, and behold, it was the wrong girl!

But remember the backstory. Jacob had cheated and deceived both his brother and his father before he fled his home. Now he was the one who had been cheated and deceived.

Leah named her third son Levi, which means "attached." She announced, "Now at last my husband will become attached to me, because I have borne him three sons" (verse 34).

Sadly, that prediction didn't come true. Jacob still loved Rachel. After three babies, all boys, Leah still hadn't won Jacob's affection. Her life situation hadn't changed. She was still in the same place with the same people, and her life was marked with the same stigma. The only thing that had changed was that she now had three little boys to chase after. For any mother who has spent a day with three rambunctious toddlers, you know how emotionally draining and crazy making that can be. I'm taking a wild guess here, but I suspect that Auntie Rachel wasn't always the first one to pitch in and lend a hand in raising Reuben, Simeon, and Levi.

When Leah found out she was pregnant a fourth time, something happened. I don't know what exactly, because the passage doesn't spell out any sort of change in Leah's heart. But I believe there was a definite shift in her perspective. Her first three boys bore names that focused on her sorrow, her less-than-desirable lot in life, her role as a victim in need of an ocean of love and attention.

My husband, the counselor, tells me that codependent people feel the need to take control of situations when things are out of control and find they can gain a position of power by getting others to feel sorry for them.

We all know people like that. More than likely, we have all *been* people like that at one time or another. Our life situations may seem unfair and chaotic. Our moods may express unhappiness and smoldering anger. We may engage in magical thinking, believing that other people will suddenly treat us differently because of something we do. But they continue treating us the way they always have. All of us have been in the place of Less-Than Leah. We have borne the name "cow." Through no fault of our own, we are where we are, and as hard as we've tried, we can't get others to treat us differently, to show us the kind of honor, love, and respect we feel we deserve.

That's when we must take our focus off ourselves and others and fix our gaze on Father God alone. I can't prove it, but I think that's what Leah did. She gave birth to her fourth son, and yet no declarations came forth about how God had seen her misery or heard that she wasn't loved. She didn't try to prove herself worthy of being attached to her husband.

She named her fourth son Judah, which means "praise." Her statement at the naming of her son seems to come from a changed heart when she said, "This time I will praise the LORD" (verse 35).

Judah. Oh, the force of that name! Oh, the power of praise! Those of us who have gone through a season of depression know that something magnificent and transforming happens when we take our eyes off ourselves and our surroundings and lift them heavenward in praise to God for all he has done. Praise opens the door to a grateful spirit.

Leah's situation didn't change. She changed. She chose to praise God and express that praise every time she said her baby boy's name—Judah. Praise.

Praise the LORD!
Oh give thanks to the LORD,
for he is good,
for his steadfast love
endures forever!
—Psalm 106:1 ESV

Did God delight in her change of heart? Did he bless her for turning her focus to him instead of continuing down her self-absorbed path of misery?

Yes, he did. When God chose the family line through which his own Son would one day be born, he didn't choose Reuben, the firstborn, who traditionally received the blessing and birthright. God didn't choose Simeon. And he didn't choose Levi.

God chose Judah as the one from whose line the Messiah would come. Leah is one of the women in the line of Christ.

The rest of the story about Jacob, Rachel, and Leah is complicated. At last Rachel had a son. She named him Joseph, which means "may he add." Perhaps she was hoping God would add more sons to her side of the tally.

God did. He gave Rachel the last of the twelve boys born to Jacob, who grew up to become the twelve tribes of Israel. That last baby boy didn't come into this world easily. He took all the strength from his mother as he made his entrance. With Rachel's final breath, she whispered the name Ben-Oni, which means "son of my sorrow." Jacob, however, changed his name to Benjamin, which means "son of my right hand."

Then Rachel, the beautiful little lamb whom Jacob adored, breathed her last and "was buried on the way to Ephrath (that is, Bethlehem)" (Genesis 35:19). Rachel's grave became the first grace marker that pointed the way to the tiny dot on this spinning planet where God's only Son would one day take his first breath of earthly air. He would be God's little lamb. He would be God's Son-of-My-Sorrow as well as God's Son-of-My-Right-Hand. He would show us grace personified, and in him and through him all of us would have the opportunity to be reconciled with the Father.

He brought this Good News of peace to you Gentiles who were far away from him, and peace to the Jews who were near. Now all of us can come to the Father through the same Holy Spirit because of what Christ has done for us.

—Ephesians 2:17–18 NLT

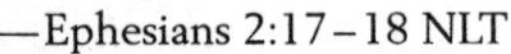

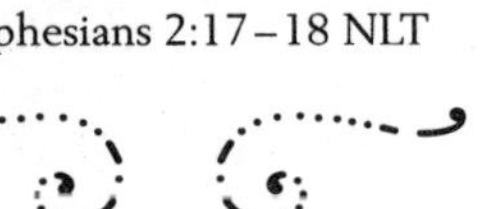

Created Anew

I thought a lot about Leah's story the January after my father had breathed his last. I read her story by the fire on my Selah Day as the heavy skies spread a coat of winter white across the Great Northwest. With a cuppa tea to warm my hands, I watched out the front window as the neighborhood kids tobogganed down the sloped side of the park across the street. The gazebo in the center of the park was still trimmed in a halo of twinkling white lights from Christmas. Behind the gazebo rose a forest of noble firs and honorable cedars that stood tall and proud, eagerly catching the enchanting snowflakes and balancing them on every branch.

My year of loss was over. I had lost my father. I had lost nearly all my book contracts. And I had also experienced the good loss of a malignant growth in my gut, as well as the poisonous weight of unforgiveness that had burrowed into my heart.

It occurred to me that if I hadn't gone through such a winnowing process of learning how to forgive from the heart, I wouldn't have been so in tune with my father's lack of peace and his need to reconcile with his brother. If I hadn't lost the writing projects, I wouldn't have been as available to spend so many days with my parents during my father's final year.

Like Leah, though, many things in my life hadn't changed. My husband and I were still having the same financial struggles, and I had the same complicated relationships and business agreements. I wondered how many of my conversations the year before had focused on my sadness, worries, and weaknesses. How many times had I tried to gain control because I viewed so much of my life as out of control? Had I sabotaged relationships with my bulldozing arrogance? Like Leah, had I tried to prove my worth by what I thought I had accomplished on my own, when really, anything I accomplished had been by God's hand of blessing?

I was quite certain I'd been a "cow" on a number of occasions.

As I contemplated the big picture of the previous year, my focus narrowed once again to the central theme of grace. I didn't deserve anything, and yet God chose to bless again and again. He gave. I received. It was all his doing.

With a renewed focus, I was ready to do the good work God had

So God can point to us in all future ages as examples of the incredible wealth of his grace and kindness toward us, as shown in all he has done for us who are united with Christ Jesus. God saved you by his grace when you believed. And you can't take credit for this; it is a gift from God. Salvation is not a reward for the good things we have done, so none of us can boast about it. For we are God's masterpiece. He has created us anew in Christ Jesus, so we can do the good things he planned for us long ago.

—Ephesians 2:7–10 NLT

created me to do. A new year stretched before me with an open schedule as unmarked as the pristine snow in our front yard. It was time to ask the Lord for a new banner word. I was ready for a change. I'm sure he was ready to bring about a change in me. Taking a clue from Leah's change of heart, I began to praise God.

Opening the journal in my lap, I wrote the first thing that came to my heart. "Oh, Great God, you are wonderful in all your ways!" Exclamations of praise and thanksgiving slid down the white pages of my new journal with gleeful abandon. Nothing about any of my life situations had changed. Yet as I thanked God for his goodness and all he had done for us over the years, joy bubbled up. Hope returned.

Instead of the usual first-of-the-year list of goals and aspirations, I wrote out praise after praise until my heart filled to overflowing gratefulness and deep, abiding awe. I told Jesus I loved him. I told him I trusted him. Completely. I wrote a rather mushy love letter to God, filled with praise.

As the candle burned low, my words, it seemed, were all spent. I closed the cover of the christened journal for the new year and felt a stirring sense of anticipation over what the Lord was going to do in the days ahead.

To express my exuberance, I rose from my cozy chair by the fire, went outside, and placed my bare feet in the fresh, crystallized snow.

I felt so alive! The time I had spent with my Savior, reconciling my spirit to his, nestling under the shadow of his wings, felt so rich and full, like a sacred, stolen moment that only he and I would understand.

Turning my face toward the heavens, I smiled a big, straight-toothed grin at my heavenly Father and gave him a wink.

The joy of the L*ORD* *is your strength.*

—Nehemiah 8:10

Chapter 8

PURE GRACE IN EVERY SEASON

You know what I long for, Lord;
you hear my every sigh.

— PSALM 38:9 NLT

Why do we welcome the change of seasons in the calendar year and yet dodge the change of seasons in our lives? We revel in the pristine beauty of winter's snowfall and bask in the warmth of summer's glow. We kick up our heels when the leaves change color and shower the earth with their fleeting glamour. And every spring we gasp with a sense of excitement when the first pale crocus pops up from the deadened earth. Each season comes with its unique beauties, unparalleled in any other season.

Yet we resist the coming of autumn, when all the leaves fall from the trees of our lives. Those trees in the summer season had grown full of green life and sweet fruit. Now, to our dismay, all that goodness is dropping around us, shriveling up and returning to where it came from. We bundle up against the stark winds and dark vacancies of winter, mourning the loss of summer's bliss, dreaming of daffodils while only seeing frost-crusted dirt.

Why are we caught off guard when the seasons change? We wonder if we've done something to precipitate the loss of the previous abundance and all the vibrant evidences of God's wonder-working power. All of nature willingly surrenders to the changes in the physical universe, yet nothing in our human nature allows us to simply let the season be what it is and trust that the hand of the Great Gardener is still at work in us, carrying out his bigger plan for the world as well as for our lives.

When I entered that pocket of grace in January by the fire and praise permeated my spirit, I was confident that God was about to do something grand, something glorious. I believed all his promises. I'd seen the rainbows of hope at the end of so much loss. I felt closer to him than I had ever been. Every morning I woke expectantly, but every night I closed my eyes still void of direction.

Nothing seemed to have changed. It was still winter.

Did this dark void of any sort of new life mean that I was finished as a writer? Were all the books going to go out of print, and that would be the end of that? If so, then what did God want me to do? What was my life supposed to be about? I asked him many times, but all I heard in my chilled heart was silence.

My spirit shivered in the bleak midwinter. My bones ached for the warmth of his presence the way I had felt the Lord's closeness in the summer season. I continued to praise him even though the feelings weren't there. It was an act of obedience. I had learned long ago that the Lord's blessing happens inside the obedience.

I wrote my life verse in my journal for that new year: "My life is worth nothing to me unless I use it for finishing the work assigned me by the Lord Jesus—the work of telling others the Good News about the wonderful grace of God" (Acts 20:24 NLT). I asked God how this mandate I felt all the way to my core might somehow be accomplished. How was I to finish, to figure out what the next assignment was? And how was I to communicate God's love and grace? All was silent from the wintery heavens.

When a tree loses its leaves and stands there in public with its bare branches exposed and stretching out every which way, that's the time the gardener does the necessary work of pruning. He uses sharp tools to accomplish the work properly. He knows exactly where to cut. Then he throws the trimmings onto the fire and burns them.

Nothing is attractive about this process. And if you happen to be a tree planted in public view, it can be rather humiliating. Especially when the pruning results in the natural response of a continual flow of sap; or in human terms—tears. Keeping in mind the words of Psalm 56:8, where it says, "You have collected all my tears in your bottle" (NLT), I often said, "Lord, it's me again. You better go get your bottle."

I spent time considering the pruning process described in John 15 where Jesus said he was "the true vine," and we are the branches. He told his disciples, "Remain in me, as I also remain in you. No branch can bear fruit by itself; it must remain in the vine.... If you remain in me and I in you, you will bear much fruit; apart from me you can do nothing" (verses 4, 5).

Jesus said it was for his Father's glory that we go through this pruning so that we will "bear much fruit." Not just some fruit or more fruit but *much* fruit. Visions of any sort of fruit seem ludicrous to the naked tree shivering in the winter wind as more and more branches are cut down and burned up.

Pierre Teilhard de Chardin, born in 1881, explained this season this way:

Above all, trust in the slow work of God.
We are quite naturally impatient in everything to reach the end without delay.

We should like to skip the intermediate stages.
We are impatient of being on the way to something unknown, something new....
Only God could say what this new spirit gradually forming within you will be.
Give our Lord the benefit of believing that his hand is leading you,
And accept the anxiety of feeling yourself in suspense and incomplete.

"In suspense and incomplete" explained how I felt during those weeks of winter in my soul. A restlessness, it seems, resides in those who long for more of Jesus. The feeling of being in suspense between here and heaven is very real. I saw this played out in my mother's life as she went through tremendous changes after my dad passed away.

Eventually we realize that we can be fulfilled and yet live out our days sensing an incompleteness until we are made complete in his presence. We live with the longing to be with him. Until that day we live with a constant anticipation of wanting something more, and whether we realize it or not, that something more is the Lord's presence.

A Kindred Victim of Grace

I wonder if this intrinsic sense of longing propelled Mary Magdalene to be among the first of Jesus' followers to venture to the garden tomb early in the morning on the third day after the crucifixion. Just before the hint of first light, she made her way to the tomb. How shocking to find that the stone had been rolled away from the opening, and the garden tomb was empty.

Mary had been there at the foot of the cross on Friday. She had watched her Savior die. After Joseph of Arimathea and Nicodemus had prepared Christ's body for burial and placed him in the tomb, they had rolled the stone in place and left. But Mary didn't leave. She lingered by the sealed tomb after the others were gone.

Was she feeling incomplete and anxious from being in suspense?

Her Lord was gone. This wasn't the way any of Jesus' followers had thought things would go. Their king was dead. How could he set up the kingdom he had talked about and all of them were waiting for?

Mary ran to tell Simon Peter about the empty tomb. Her breathless words to him were, "They have taken the Lord out of the tomb, and we don't know where they have put him!" (John 20:2). If she had an inkling that the foretold resurrection had taken place, she didn't add this possibility to her conclusion. She assumed the Lord's body had been stolen, and she didn't know where to find it.

Peter and John ran to the tomb and found the strips of linen that Nicodemus and Joseph of Arimathea had wrapped Christ's body in. The burial cloth that had been around Jesus' head was folded up by itself, separate from the linen. This was such a small detail, yet it was the turning point for "the disciple whom Jesus loved." John stated that at that moment he believed. The meaning of the Scriptures was suddenly clear to him. Jesus had risen from the dead. He was the Son of God!

John had seen miracles and heard the Lord speak truth for three years, yet this was the moment he believed. Was it the way the linen strips were lying in the tomb that made it clear this hadn't been the work of grave robbers? Clearly thieves don't clean up after themselves or take time to fold a burial cloth in a certain way.

After all the meals they had shared, all the miles they had walked together, all the conversations they had had over those years, John knew Christ well. Could it be that John recognized something familiar in the way the burial cloth was folded? Had he seen the Lord fold blankets and cloaks so many times that he knew no one else but Jesus could have folded the cloth this way?

The longer we walk with the Lord, the more we recognize his distinct ways of doing things. We see touches in our lives as subtle as the way the burial cloth was folded, and we believe. We believe that what is happening in the midst of the shock and terror of the moment has Jesus' fingerprints all over it. He did this for a specific purpose.

We can't see him. We don't understand why. But we see evidence of his presence, of his hand at work in the situation, and we believe. We believe he is the Son of God and he has power over everything, including death.

What happened next is one of my favorite scenes in the New Testament. An angel appeared at the tomb and told the small clutch of Jesus' friends not to be afraid. Jesus had risen! Just as he said he would.

Whether that announcement confounded or comforted them, Peter and John went on their way. By Jewish tradition they had been in very deep mourning since sundown on the Sabbath. And yet their mourning had suddenly been interrupted at the tomb. John somehow believed that Jesus was alive when he saw the empty tomb and the folded grave clothes.

Now what? The last time Jesus had spoken to them, he told them that he was the vine and they were the branches; they needed to abide in him. Jesus had prayed that they would be one even as he and his Father were one. He had called them his "friends," since a servant didn't know what his master was doing.

Yet they didn't know what he was doing. There they were, emotionally spent, severed from the True Vine who had been with them every moment for many years, and now an angel had told them he was risen. But where was he? Where did he go? Where did they have to go to see him again?

They didn't know what to do, so they went home.

Mary Magdalene, however, didn't leave. She stayed just as she had stayed at the foot of the cross. Just as she had lingered in the garden after the stone had been rolled into place, sealing the tomb with her Savior's body inside. And now, just like Eve, Mary was waiting in a garden for God to make his next move.

I love this glimpse of a relentless woman longing for her Savior. Nothing made sense, but she wasn't giving up. She wasn't moving.

Thousands had followed Jesus throughout Judea. He fed them,

healed them, instructed them, forgave them, and he wept over them because of his deep love for them. Only a week earlier, hundreds of his followers welcomed him into Jerusalem with shouts of praise. Now everything, according to their view of events, had gone terribly wrong. All hope was lost. They left. All of them had gone home.

All but Mary Magdalene. Mary, the woman from whom Jesus had cast out seven demons. She knew what it was like to be separated from God. She knew pain, sorrow, emptiness, torture, and the very face of evil. She also knew love. God's perfect and complete love made flesh in his only Son.

That morning at the empty tomb, Mary didn't go home with Peter and John. She stayed put, longing for Jesus and lingering at the tomb. Mary wept. Her emotions were spent; her vision was blurred. All she knew was that she wanted Jesus back.

This feels like a parallel to the opening scene at the beginning of God's Story. In that garden the Lord God was the one who tarried in the cool of the day. He knew all that had been shattered in the fall. His first love had been taken from him. Yet, as a Relentless Lover, he came back to the garden seeking his first love. He called out to them with a question, "Where are you?" (Genesis 3:9).

Now, at this pivotal moment in God's Great Story, the scene at the tomb was a garden once again. This time one of his children came to the garden, not in the cool of the day, but at first light. Mary arrived at the beginning of a new morn, a new era. She didn't know it yet, but it was opening day of the greatest surprise gift that God had been waiting to give his beloved. It was Reconciliation Day! And Mary was the first in line.

Jesus was there. He was right there in the midst of her deep sorrow, confusion, and loss. Through her tear-clouded eyes, she looked up and assumed he was the gardener.

Then he spoke to her, "Woman, why are you crying? Who is it you are looking for?" (John 20:15).

Mary didn't recognize his voice. Was it because her ears were throbbing with emotion and her hearing had become as clouded as her tear-blurred vision? Or had Jesus changed so much as the risen Lord that his whole image had been completely transformed?

Why did Mary think he was the gardener? Was it because of what he was wearing? Jesus had put aside the burial clothes, nice and tidy. But he needed something to wear, and God must have provided. In the first garden after the resident gardeners disobeyed, they were in need of something to wear. God himself initiated the first death when he took an animal's life to provide suitable coverings for them. On resurrection day, Christ, the Son of God who obeyed his Father and accomplished the final sacrificial death, was also in need of something to wear. The Father could have provided anything for his Son. What he chose were the coverings of the resident gardener.

What a full circle.

And now another full circle is about to take place. It seems as if the great echo of God's question in the garden so long ago was at last returning to his ears after all these millennia. The Relentless Lover called out to Adam and Eve, "Where are you?" Here, in this second garden, Mary responded by saying, in essence, "Where is he? I want him back."

How many centuries God had waited! How many millions of his children had he pursued with his unfailing love and mercy? How few of those free-will-infused children had ever responded in kind and turned to him with their whole hearts? How tiny is the number of those who have lingered long after all the other devoted followers have gone home.

Mary's determination to be reunited with her Lord was fierce. She even said, "Tell me where you have put him, and I will get him" (verse 15).

Now Mary, how were you going to carry the body of a fully-grown man that had been embalmed with one hundred pounds of oils and spices? And if you had gotten him, where were you going to put him? Back in the tomb?

Mary had a deep, abiding love for the Lord. She was passionate, not rational. All she knew was that she wanted him back.

Jesus spoke one word to Mary. She had been hunched down, peering into the tomb and sobbing when he spoke that one word. When she heard it, she pulled herself together and turned fully toward him. The one word Jesus spoke was her name: "Mary."

Raised to New Life

What if you knew that in the midst of your most devastating tragedy, Jesus was right there, even if you didn't recognize his voice or see his specific touches in the details of your heartbreaking situation? What if, in your most painful, hunched-over, sobbing moments, you knew that he knew you by name? Would you turn fully toward him as Mary did?

In the silent winter of my life, I wanted to believe that Jesus was right there with me. I wanted to believe that he hadn't forgotten me. That he knew me by name and knew what he was doing. He was, indeed, a Gardener during those dark months, uncompromising as he continued the task of chopping off anything in my life that didn't honor him. That's really all I knew at the time.

This is what the
LORD says—
he who created you, Jacob,
he who formed you, Israel:
"Do not fear, for I have
redeemed you;
I have summoned you
by name; you are mine."
—Isaiah 43:1

I wanted to be one who lingered.

As the horrid pruning went on, I slipped in and out of melancholy. I had felt such strength and joy when my days were filled with thanksgiving and praise. But as soon as I stopped being grateful for everything the Lord was doing, whether I understood it or not, my thoughts quickly focused on my needs. And I began to stagnate.

I felt strangely warm and filled when people felt sorry for me regarding all my losses—the obvious ones as well as the ones I was so willing to tell them about. I liked giving myself permission to host yet another pity party during which I was the guest of honor. I found it easy to take offense at things others said and did whenever it felt abrasive to my sensitive spirit. How quickly I let go of all hope.

Instead of lingering at the foot of the cross or by the stone that was rolled away, instead of waiting with passionate expectation to see what God was going to do now, I went home to my old nature. Back to a closed-in place with Fear and Doubt. I curled up inside a loneliness that made my bones shiver.

Then one day, when I least expected it and certainly didn't deserve it, I became a victim of grace once again. God gave me a gift that was delivered at just the right time.

My literary agent, Janet, called me. "How would you like to write a novel for the Women of Faith?"

All of my creative juices began to flow again. Fresh, new idea buds popped out on the stubby branches that had been pruned, and before my eyes I saw what happens when the Lord unleashes his resurrection power. All kinds of sprigs, twigs, and blossoms sprouted at once.

I wait for the LORD,
my whole being waits, and
in his word I put my hope.

—Psalm 130:5

The seasons had changed, as they always do. Springtime had returned by God's hand and faithfulness, not by anything I had done to try to speed the winter along. I knew that God didn't love me any less because of my small-hearted, weak-spirited attitude that centered on my inconveniences during that fallow season. Yet I wished I had waited for him with my whole heart. I wished I had lingered with more passion for his presence and a more fervent hope.

I dove into writing a book proposal for the Women of Faith novel and pulled from all the wacky adventures my forever friend, Donna, and I had experienced during our trip to Europe. I thought about our time in Latvia, where we met Mary, who had such a sweet love for Corrie ten Boom, and about the trip to Finland, where we stayed with the editor from the Christian publishing house that had translated the first few Christy Miller books into Finnish. We had gone to Helsinki in winter, and one of the grand and comical highlights of that trip was venturing into an authentic Finnish sauna and then running outside and rolling in the snow.

When I turned in the summary for the Women of Faith novel, the working title was *Fat Chicks in a Finnish Sauna*. Chick lit was just coming on the scene, and I thought it would be fun to write in such a way that the characters could be portrayed as best friends in midlife who were experiencing new adventures that God had opened up to them. It was supposed to be a bit lighthearted.

The title for that book didn't grab the team at Women of Faith. They were thinking that with my experience in writing teen fiction, I might write something about mothers and daughters. They wanted a more layered novel about relationships.

I remember the sunny afternoon when Janet gave me that information on the phone. I went out to the backyard and pulled the hammock onto the grass. As I stretched out under a rare, clear blue Northwest sky, I thought about the first time Janet had called me. I was standing in the driveway with my eight-month-old daughter on my hip and my five-year-old son spinning circles on his tricycle in the driveway. Janet had been the editor at that first publishing house that decided to take a chance and publish my first Christy Miller novel. Now she was my agent and a longtime friend.

As I swayed in the hammock, a simple line came into my thoughts: *Everybody has a story, honey girl. You listen to their story, and your story will come and find you.*

I suddenly knew I had the opening line for a book that would be a mother-daughter journey to Louisiana to see the family's matriarch. I had already done the research when my daughter was twelve and she and I had driven our family van from Portland, Oregon, to a small town east of Shreveport, Louisiana, to visit my grandmother, whom all the relatives in the South called "Great Lady."

The story tumbled out as I returned to the regimen of rising three days a week at 3:00 a.m. and writing my heart out. More springtime good news sprouted. The publisher of the Glenbrooke series wanted to pick up the Christy Miller and Sierra Jensen books for publication. They planned to repackage the two series and rerelease them in hardcover, with a collection of three novels in each volume.

I cried like spring rain when I heard the news. The stories that I thought were done—dead and gone—were being resurrected and made available for a new generation of readers. Once again I was seeing God fulfill the verse he had put in my mind so many years ago: "Let this be written for a future generation, that a people not yet created may praise the LORD" (Psalm 102:18).

As if all that weren't enough great news, the same publisher was interested in hearing about what I wanted to write next. I told them about the *Fat Chicks* book idea, and the editor busted up. The title could easily offend, so the editor said that if I came up with a different title, he would be happy to champion the idea to the publishing committee to see what might happen.

I didn't give much thought to coming up with a new title for the book about the midlife friends visiting Finland. All my focus was on *Gardenias for Breakfast*, the Women of Faith novel I was writing. I couldn't miss the deadline because the book was scheduled to be promoted and sold at their events, and I had been invited to travel to five of those events to sign copies. It was all very exciting. New life, new growth, new stories. Same faithful Lord Jesus, the Author and Finisher of my faith.

I was listening to his Great Story when my story came and found me.

Summer followed spring that year, as it always does, due to God's faithfulness. On a particularly sunny day, I met up with Donna, and the two of us took our beach chairs and set them up on a strip of sand along the Columbia River. We were wearing shorts and were eager to absorb our overdue supply of vitamin D via our white arms and legs. The topic of conversation turned to girlfriend subjects, such as our underarm flab.

"Mine is wobblier than yours," Donna claimed.

"No way. Look, mine is much worse," I insisted.

"Oh yeah? Well, if you want to have a real competition, let's compare varicose veins. Mine are double yours. No, triple."

"Not even close. Look. And here too. And this leg is like a map of a major freeway system."

With all our lumpy, bumpy, wobbly, wiggly comparisons came a lot of laughter. Donna and I could always count on each other for laughter. We had met when our babies were babies, and we grew up with them and each other. Her eldest daughter was now married, and here we were, still enjoying the blessing of being besties.

"What are we?" I asked. "Are we best friends? Do you still have a best friend when you're this old?"

"We're more like sisters," she said.

"Yeah, but I want to think we still got it goin' on, varicose veins and everything."

"Agreed. We're still a couple of chicks," Donna said.

"We're Sisterchicks!"

Oh, that we might know the LORD!
Let us press on to know him.
He will respond to us as surely as the arrival of dawn
or the coming of rains in early spring.

—Hosea 6:3 NLT

Donna pointed at me. "Write that down. Now! You're gonna want that word one day. That's the perfect word to describe us. More than friends. Sisterchicks. That's it. Right there."

I didn't need to write down the word. It was embedded in me as the new title for the book about the trip Donna and I had taken to Finland. There it was, delivered to me on that sunny afternoon: *Sisterchicks® on the Loose!*

The publisher agreed that was the title they wanted to go with. A contract was in the works. They had only one question for me: How quickly could I write this new book?

I was a giddy sisterchick, basking in the summertime sun of God's grace.

Chapter 9

DARE TO DREAM AGAIN

This is the LORD*'s doing;*
it is marvelous in our eyes.

—PSALM 118:23 ESV

I was pushing the cart down the cereal aisle at the grocery store when one of our neighbors spotted me and came rushing toward me. "Did you see your book? It's in the paper!"

"No, I didn't see it. Which newspaper?"

"*USA Today.* It's on the cover of the entertainment section. The article said that *Sisterchicks on the Loose!* has launched a whole new genre of women's fiction in the Christian market."

I knew that wasn't true; my book hadn't launched a new genre. Other writers were publishing novels at this time that fell into the chick-lit category, but somehow mine landed in the spotlight. The media attention to the book had been noticed, and a rush of enthusiasm followed. The publisher asked for more books in the series. They wanted the stories to feature midlife friends exploring other parts of the world. These women would share madcap adventures in interesting places while they discovered that God was much bigger than they ever realized.

I was off and running. The location for the second book was easy to choose: Hawaii. My in-laws owned a vacation rental condo there, and ever since my husband and I honeymooned in the islands, we returned to Hawaii every chance we got. We even spent a school year on Maui when our son was in third grade. We loved everything about Hawaii, and after so many visits, I found it easy to come up with the plot for the second Sisterchicks novel. I wanted to write about two former college roommates reuniting and fulfilling a dream to visit Hawaii.

As I wrote *Sisterchicks Do the Hula!*, I tried to imagine what it would be like to reunite with my old college roomie and rent a convertible so we could tootle around the island and catch up with each other's lives. Marjie and I hadn't seen each other in years. Our communication was down to exchanging Christmas cards each year, along with a family photo and update letter. During our college years, we had shared so many dreams. I wrote those thoughts and feelings into the Sisterchicks novels, and soon these stories resonated with thousands of other women in midlife who were looking for some encouragement and a nudge to trust God in a new way and even dare to dream again.

Now all glory to God, who is able, through his mighty power at work within us, to accomplish infinitely more than we might ask or think.

—Ephesians 3:20 NLT

For the third Sisterchicks book, a cruise to Mexico was the setting, because a woman who used to work in publishing and was now in the travel industry had given my agent, Janet, and I a free cruise package. I felt that God was making dreams come true right and left. I hadn't asked for this, but he was lavishly giving me more than I dared to wish for.

So many amazing things were happening at once. I was traveling to the Women of Faith events that year, where I signed copies of *Gardenias for Breakfast* and met women who had just read the first Sisterchicks novels and were asking for more.

The Christy Miller and Sierra Jensen series were rereleased in hardcover by the new publisher, and a whole new generation of teens was discovering the Forever Friends characters. My inbox filled with emails from young girls who were giving their lives to Christ after reading these books. Midlife mamas were writing to tell me sweet ways that the Lord was using the Sisterchicks books to prompt them to go deeper in their friendships, to be reunited with old friends, or to renew their belief in dreams.

The Glenbrooke stories were given new covers and a boost when the series was picked up by grocery stores. Women who would never have found their way to a Christian bookstore or a women's group at a church were finding these books and taking in the truth about God's love and care for them as they saw it demonstrated in the characters' lives.

Never would I have expected the bountiful, fragrant season of new life and springtime blossoming that God, in his resurrection power, was bringing about. The adventures and opportunities on the writing front couldn't have gotten any better—but they did.

After the third Sisterchicks book was completed, the publisher asked if I would write three more books in the series. Then they changed the number and said, "No, would you write five more for a series of eight books?"

With enthusiasm we discussed the possible locations for these stories: Australia, Paris, Venice, London, Amsterdam. Wow! Yes, please. My husband was in on that meeting, and he said to the publisher, "If you want Robin to write authentically about these places, you really should send her there to do the research before she starts to write."

The folks in the meeting looked at each other and said, "Okay, we can do that. Your sales are strong enough on the first books in the series. We'll give you a travel budget, and you may go to all these places before you write about them."

I couldn't believe it! The travel budget and the opportunity to write books set in those exotic locations was way beyond anything I ever had hoped or dreamed. It was exactly what I had wished for as a young woman—to travel around the world and tell people about God's love and grace.

God was accomplishing his purposes, and I was the immensely willing victim of his extravagant grace.

The stories I had been writing for more than twenty years were being translated into various languages and were "traveling" around the world with the message of God's love and grace. Now God was sending me around the world. Over the next few years, God did some amazing things as he poured out grace upon grace on me. The travel budget covered airfare and several nights in a hotel. On each trip the Lord seemed to multiply the opportunities so that I was able to experience oh so much more than what it looked like on paper.

In Venice, my longtime friend Ruby and I stayed in a restored, fifteenth-century palace, complete with masterpiece paintings on the ceilings and huge shuttered windows that opened up to an attached balcony over a quiet canal. We took a gondola ride and attended early morning vespers sung by Benedictine monks on San Giorgio island. At San Marcos Square, we fed pigeons and sampled a dozen varieties of gelato.

In London my Sisterchicks Julee and Marion and I took a bus to Oxford and visited the Kilns, C. S. Lewis's home. We stood in front of the window he had looked out in those "dewy, cobwebby hours" of the morning with his cup of tea as he answered his correspondence by hand. We visited the church he attended for forty years, and I sat in the pew in the same spot where he had sat each week. To top it off, we met with other British authors and had afternoon tea at the Ritz. With our pinkies up, of course.

In the Netherlands, the home of my Forever Friend Anne, I tried on wooden shoes and scooped up armfuls of colorful tulips. She introduced me to Dutch delights, such as *pannekoeken* and *stroopwafels* and filled me in on more tales of Corrie ten Boom and her family.

In Paris, I scaled the Eiffel Tower and sang at the top of my lungs on a gorgeous summer's eve. I met Mona Lisa eyeball to eyeball at the Louvre and sipped *café* on the Champs-Elysées.

Every corner I explored with a special Sisterchick was filled with the mystery and beauty of God's presence and covered by his grace.

The sweetest unexpected gift was when I was in Australia. The publisher who distributes my books Down Under took me to a preserve outside of Sydney where a childhood dream of mine was fulfilled to the last detail. I fed a kangaroo out of the palm of my hand. She had a little joey in her pouch, and her tongue felt dry as she lapped up the Cheerios I held out to her. As a child I had imagined that kangaroos were in the same camp as unicorns. They couldn't possibly be real. But there in front of me was a very real kangaroo, and she was eating out of the palm of my hand.

Why was the Lord bestowing so much grace on me? I was finding myself with an embarrassing abundance of riches. The principle of Luke 12:48 seemed to follow me around: "When someone has been given much, much will be required in return" (NLT).

How was I supposed to turn around and give back "much" out of the riches that were raining down on me? I was rich, rich, rich in grace, and that's when I discovered the purpose of blessings: God blesses us so that we can bless others. As God promised Abraham, "I will bless you ... and you will be a blessing" (Genesis 12:2).

It was my turn to make others the victims of grace.

They didn't see the blessings coming. They didn't do anything to deserve them. I was learning to give in the same way God had given to me, extravagantly.

Looking back now, I see how few times the grace giving was expressed with dollars. Our family gave readily of what we had, but the Lord was teaching us to give the way he did. Whenever we had deep personal needs and longings, rarely had the Lord thrown money at the problems and called that the final solution. He always provided our daily bread, but the real gifts of his grace had come in more eternal ways.

God loved me when I didn't deserve to be loved. He forgave me when I had betrayed and disobeyed him. He showed me his true love and friendship by being present and by bringing people into my life who were an encouragement. And I was to give back in the same way out of the abundance he had given me. I gave time to others who wanted to learn how to use their gifts of storytelling. I set aside time to answer mail from readers. We opened our home to a number of young people who needed a place to live but had no money for rent. We kept whatever income we needed to pay the bills and let go of the rest.

A few years earlier, Media Associates International (MAI) had invited me to speak at one of their international LittWorld conferences in the Philippines, but I wasn't able to go because of my father's medical condition. I was invited again to their triennial conference, and again I had to decline because of my father's situation.

When MAI extended yet another invitation, this time I was able to accept. The LittWorld conference was to be held in Brazil, and I was very excited because the Christy Miller and Sierra Jensen books had been translated into Portuguese and were popular with many teens in Brazil. My husband and I made plans to go together, and I contacted the publisher in Brazil to see if we could set up some speaking events with churches, schools, and youth groups. We had six months to plan, so it looked as if we would be able to accomplish much on this trip.

In the midst of the planning, I was invited to join the MAI board of directors, and I enthusiastically accepted. In every way this opportunity felt like the exponential fulfilling of those original dreams God had planted in my heart long ago. I hadn't traveled around the world as a missionary. Instead, as Wambura so poignantly told me when she and I met at the first LittWorld conference I attended in England, the books I was writing were the missionaries. They were traveling around the world, and God was using them to tell others about his love and grace.

But God's plans are full-circle plans. He had arranged for my books to travel around the world, and now he was arranging ways for me to travel around the world as well, delighting in God's amazing creation and crafting stories that reflected his beauty.

I experienced an even greater full circle when the Lord opened the door for me to participate with MAI and help facilitate the training of writers around the world. I was able to impart to others the basics of writing so they could hone their storytelling gifts and write books in their heart languages. Those books would become the undercover missionaries that would travel through their countries and cultures, telling people of God's love and grace.

This was so much greater than any small dream I had ever imagined.

A Kindred Victim of Grace

So which woman in the Bible did I find it easiest to relate to during this season of abundant harvest? My kindred victim of grace was a woman who traveled to another country and immersed herself in their culture. She spent a life-changing night on a threshing floor, silently watching the ancient stars over Bethlehem.

Her name is Ruth, which means "friend," and she was indeed a wonderful friend to her mother-in-law, Naomi.

During a time of famine in the land of Israel, Naomi, her husband, and her two sons left Bethlehem—which means "House of Bread"—

and moved to Moab, a dry, rocky region outside the Promised Land. Moab is the region where Moses had gazed out over the Promised Land but wasn't allowed to enter, and where he later died on Mount Nebo.

In Psalm 60:8 God called Moab his "washbasin." Nothing good is said about Moab in all of Scripture. The worst part about the land of Moab was the gods the people of that region worshipped. Archaeologists have found evidence of the false deities Chemosh and Molech in excavations of this pagan land. The Moabite gods were cast as bronze idols and set on fire until they were heated to an unbearable degree. Then an infant would be placed in their arms, offered as a human sacrifice.

Naomi and her family left the House of Bread and went to live in the washbasin. Scripture doesn't tell us whether that was a good decision. Those who have ever been in a place of abundance and then find themselves in a time of famine understand what it's like to go searching for food when all the usual streams of provision have dried up. The reason Naomi and her family moved to Moab seems to have been the assurance of provisions and perhaps a better life.

But after almost ten years in this pagan land, Naomi's husband and both of her sons had died. This Israelite family had left the circle of friends and family who worshipped the true and living God and had become enmeshed in a place where the abomination of human sacrifice was part of the culture. Both of Naomi's sons had married women from Moab, which was also something God had commanded his people not to do.

Nothing had gone the way Naomi and her husband had hoped, and now Naomi had been left as a widow with her two Moabite daughters-in-law. She had no husband, no sons, and no grandchildren. The famine that scorched Bethlehem had seared her life.

But the seasons changed, as they always do. Faithful God extended his grace to this grieving woman. He made his rain to come down on the just and the unjust, and Naomi's hope was renewed when she received news that the drought in Judea had ended. The Lord had blessed his people, and the House of Bread was once more a place of grain, harvest, and hope. So Naomi returned to Bethlehem, and her two daughters-in-law followed along.

However, Naomi didn't welcome their company. "Return home, my daughters," she told the young widows. "It is more bitter for me than for you, because the LORD's hand has turned against me!" (Ruth 1:11, 13).

Naomi, whose name means "pleasant," had been crushed under the weight of so much loss. She believed that God had removed his blessing from her and had cursed her. This severe pruning in her life was too much, and as is often the case with so much pain, hurt people hurt people. Hurting Naomi was pushing away the two women who were trying to express their support and were doing so at great sacrifice.

After many tears and hugs, the first daughter-in-law released her ties on Naomi and returned home. Who could blame her for leaving? No one wants to be around a person who is bitter and empty and rejects you even when you're trying to do what's right.

Ruth, however, "clung" to Naomi (verse 14).

"Look," Naomi said, "your sister-in-law is going back to her people and her gods. Go back with her" (verse 15).

Ruth's reply has become a classic portion of Scripture. It's often used in wedding ceremonies, even though these words were spoken from the heart of one broken woman to another. Imagine a young widow making this heartfelt vow to her embittered mother-in-law who was trying to convince her to go away:

> Don't urge me to leave you or to turn back from you. Where you go I will go, and where you stay I will stay. Your people will be my people and your God my God. Where you die I will die, and there I will be buried. May the LORD deal with me, be it ever so severely, if even death separates you and me.
>
> — RUTH 1:16 – 17

Ruth was ready to denounce the detestable gods of Moab that required human sacrifice—the vile and wicked false deities that had no power. She was ready to leave all that was familiar in Moab and enter the Promised Land, where the true God, Jehovah, would be her God. Ruth believed.

It must have been clear to Naomi that Ruth wasn't going to give up. The two women began the thirty-two-mile journey by foot over the rocky, arid roads that led back to Bethlehem.

I love that Bethlehem was their final destination, don't you? They most likely passed by Rachel's burial place on the way to Bethlehem. Many centuries later, Mary and Joseph would also journey to Bethlehem over equally treacherous roads, fraught with bandits, harsh elements, and desert creatures. Mary would make the trek full, very full, as she carried in her body the promised gift of the Messiah, God incarnate.

In stark contrast Ruth and Naomi made the journey empty. Very empty. Both of them widows. Both of them with no children. Both of them desperate for God to come and be with them and provide for them. Both of them in the midst of a harsh winter season of life and yet willing to take the risk of leaving Moab behind so that they might dare to dream again.

Ruth was clearly the more hopeful of the two women when they arrived in Bethlehem. The whole town was stirred by their arrival, but the townspeople barely recognized Naomi. The years in Moab had altered her. Naomi made it clear that her time away from her home hadn't produced anything good. She told her people no longer to call her Naomi, which means "pleasant," but to call her Mara, which means "bitter."

She then declared that she "went away full, but the LORD has brought me back empty" (verse 21).

Had Naomi forgotten the famine that prompted her family to leave Bethlehem? Certainly her belly wasn't full when she left. But her heart was full. She had a husband, two sons, and a future they were trying to build with hopes of provision, life, and grandbabies. Now she had nothing. Or did she?

I feel for Ruth at this point. She left everything and made the long journey on foot with this bitter woman. Yet when they arrived in Bethlehem, Naomi seemed to discredit the one hope she had left. Ruth, a dedicated daughter-in-law, had demonstrated her friendship but received nothing in return, not even an acknowledgment.

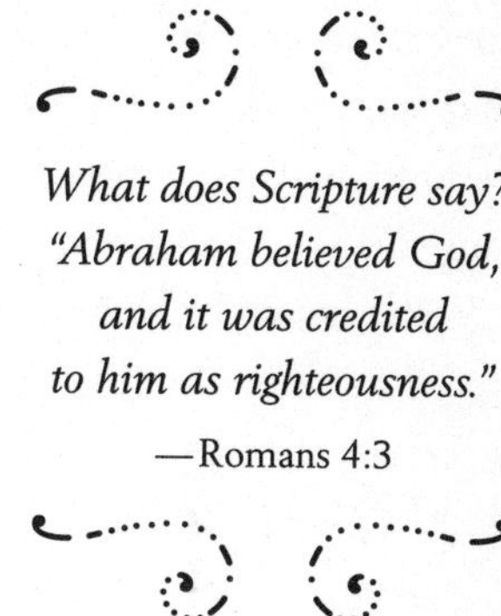

What does Scripture say? "Abraham believed God, and it was credited to him as righteousness."

—Romans 4:3

If you've ever been around bitter people, you know how their toxic attitudes can make you sick inside. You know that no matter what you do or how hard you try, your efforts will never be enough. How different the tone would have been if Naomi's announcement upon her arrival in Bethlehem had been, "Yes, I'm back. The past ten years have been devastating, but at least the Lord has provided me with this faithful friend to accompany me."

In the same way God prompted Rebekah to go to the well right when she did so that Abram's servant would notice her, it appears that God was nudging Ruth along too. And just as Hagar obeyed when the Lord directed her to return to Sarai and Leah hung in there with so little affection from Jacob, Ruth stuck to her commitment to stay with Naomi. Naomi's people had become Ruth's people, and Ruth was trusting in Naomi's God—the Living God.

The last verse in this chapter of Ruth is such a beautiful, ever-so-subtle hint at what God was about to do: "[Naomi and Ruth] arrived in Bethlehem just when people were beginning to harvest the barley" (verse 22 NIrV). It could be read as a simple, insignificant fact on first glance. But none of God's words is wasted. As a storyteller he foreshadows that something intriguing is about to happen.

"They arrived in Bethlehem just when *people* were beginning to harvest the barley" (verse 22 NIrV).

Hmm. What *people*? It reminds me of when my daughter was young and would report on a school outing or a church social event, and she would say, "Some boys from my class were there." Hmm. What *boys*? Which particular one had his eye on you? More importantly, which one did you watch the whole time?

It's a lovely little hint at the end of this first chapter and leads to the more practical question of: How were Ruth and Naomi going to be affected by the harvest? They were ready to have their bellies filled … and their hearts filled as well. How would God provide for them?

I will find my rest in God alone. He is the One who gives me hope.
—Psalm 62:5 NIrV

Like Naomi, we can be in a desolate season of our lives and in such deep sorrow that we don't even acknowledge those around us who are trying to help us. We can be as lost, hurting, and overlooked as Ruth and still be right on the verge of becoming victims of God's grace. The beautiful part is watching a young woman, a recent widow, who made a commitment and then, in spite of all the hurt, kept that commitment. Ruth didn't give up when life became more difficult. She didn't lose her patience with Naomi and walk out of her life. She stuck with her and put Naomi's best interests before her own.

As I was writing the Sisterchicks novels and exploring this sort of faithful kindness in friendships between women, I heard from readers how rare this kind of friendship really is. My heart grew heavy as I read letters from women wishing, longing, crying out for one single friend who wouldn't betray their confidence. A friend who wouldn't leave them when they were in deep, dark winter seasons, who wouldn't turn her back on them at the end of a long and difficult journey. Many times over I was told that the sort of friendships portrayed in novels were few and far between.

Some women took the Sisterchicks stories to heart, and like Ruth, they set out to be the sort of friends they always wished they had. They were the ones who made the decision to hang in there with a friend who was experiencing a time of trauma and loss. They were the ones who chose hope over despair and anticipated that the Lord was about to do a new thing in their lives.

One woman wrote to say that she had been inspired by the story of the longtime pen pals in *Sisterchicks in Wooden Shoes!* She had been corresponding with a pen pal in Australia since elementary school, and now they were in their sixties but had never met. When she read about the characters Summer and Noelle meeting for the first time in the Netherlands, this reader booked a flight, and a few months later, she and her best friend of fifty years met for the first time in Sydney. All kinds of good things came from that encounter. I should say, all kinds of "God things" tumbled out of that encounter. God richly rewarded the faithfulness and kindness of those two friends.

Another letter came from two younger women who told me how they had read the Sisterchicks books with a new friend. The three of them opened up to each other and took their book-club acquaintance to a deeper level. They were like the threefold cord in Ecclesiastes 4:12 that is "not easily broken" (NLT). They became so supportive and close that when the new friend, Karen, started having health problems, the other two Sisterchicks were there for her. Karen was single and had no family to speak of. If it hadn't been for these other two friends connecting with her through the book club, she would have been very much alone as she walked through the valley of the shadow of death.

The two Sisterchicks told me that as a result of reading the books, Karen had trusted Christ as her Savior. When the Lord took her last breath, she was ready. She had left instructions that she wanted to be buried in her Sisterchicks T-shirt because the words printed on the shirt were "Sisterchicks Forever," and for Karen, her newfound relationship with the Lord and with her two Sisterchicks was indeed forever.

Ruth also experienced a forever change in her life as a result of God's unfailing kindness and love. She made the choice to leave Moab and the false gods of that region and undertake the difficult journey to Bethlehem with Naomi. She remained a faithful and true friend in spite of the lack of affirmation from Naomi. And in the midst of all this, God orchestrated the unexpected and accomplished his purposes for Ruth.

As the next chapter of Ruth and Naomi's story opens, we are introduced to the hero in this tale—Boaz. He was a God-honoring man who happened to own one of those barley fields alluded to at the end of chapter 1. Boaz was a distant relative of Ruth's deceased father-in-law, and that put him in a position to be the "kinsman-redeemer" who could protect widows and orphans who were related to him, if he chose to do so.

Ruth didn't know those particulars when she suggested to Naomi that she go out into the fields and pick the leftover grain from the harvest. Gleaning was the provision spelled out in the law of Moses for widows, who would trail along after the harvesters and gather what was left to make their own bread.

What Ruth was offering to do was dangerous. She was a foreigner, and what she proposed doing wasn't far removed from begging. But when Ruth offered to perform this labor on behalf of both of them Naomi sent Ruth on her way. Naomi didn't give Ruth any instructions, cautions, or warnings beforehand. Only after Ruth had returned from the fields did Naomi say that she could have been harmed.

When Ruth went out to the fields to glean that morning, she was out there on her own. And yet, "as it turned out, she was working in a field belonging to Boaz" (Ruth 2:3).

This was God's protection, his provision. This was no coincidence.

Can't you almost see God wink here as you read these words? Ruth just so happened to end up in the field of Boaz, the "boy" who has his eye on her at this group event.

Think of how many times you just happened to be in a certain place at a certain time, and "as it turned out," you were exactly where God wanted you. He was the one who led you there. You ended up in that place for a purpose, so that he might write the next chapter in his Forever Tale.

As Ruth labored in the field, Boaz noticed her and asked one of the foremen about her. He reported that she was from Moab, that she had returned to Bethlehem with Naomi, and that she had been working hard all day, except for one short rest. Once again, faithfulness, hard work, and acts of selfless servanthood are noted in God's story. Like Rebekah, Ruth kept her word and did the hard work without expecting a reward. But God knew. And Boaz noticed.

As the story unfolds from here, the Lord's blessing and kindness are consistently mentioned. Boaz invited Ruth to glean only in his fields, and he let her know that he was aware of all she had done in leaving her family in Moab and coming alongside Naomi to support her.

Others may not have noticed or mentioned this, but Boaz did. And he told Ruth, "May the LORD repay you for what you have done." But Boaz didn't stop there. He kept affirming her: "May you be richly rewarded by the LORD, the God of Israel, under whose wings you have come to take refuge" (verse 12).

What a poetic and comforting image this must have been to Ruth. The gods of Moab had no wings under which a foreigner might take refuge. They had fiery arms in which infants were placed, and devoted followers would stand back and watch as a tiny human life was mercilessly taken.

By contrast, Boaz, the kinsman-redeemer, spoke to Ruth of comfort, protection, and blessings. This covering came from the God of Israel and was extended to her without hesitation and without regard for where she came from. She was welcomed into the tribe of God followers. And she was covered. Protected.

The next scene in this little novella opens with Naomi coming up with a plan. If a cartoonist had illustrated this opening scene, Naomi would have been looking at Ruth, with a shining lightbulb over Naomi's head. It seems as if Naomi had taken the focus off herself and was now paying attention to Ruth and her needs.

I have loved you with an everlasting love;
I have drawn you with unfailing kindness.

—Jeremiah 31:3

This often happens once people have worked through intense pain and loss in their lives. They can finally see through the thick fog that shrouded them when they entered that dark place. All around them a world of people and possibilities begin to come into view. This is what hope does. This is what being surrounded by God's people does. This is what it means to be covered by God's grace.

Naomi focused on Ruth's needs when she said, "I must find a home for you" (3:1).

It's true that if Ruth found a husband and was taken into his home, it would benefit Naomi as well. The motives of this mother-in-law might not have been entirely selfless, but it's quite a step up from their arrival in Bethlehem when Naomi declared that she had returned "empty," and yet Ruth was standing right there next to her, overlooked. Now Naomi was looking at Ruth, trying to figure out how a certain man named Boaz might give Ruth a second look as well.

Ruth demonstrated her servant's heart toward Naomi once again and agreed to Naomi's plan to, in essence, propose to Boaz. The way we might say it in today's vernacular would be that Ruth agreed to "put herself out there" so that Boaz would have plenty of opportunity to respond in his legal position as a kinsman-redeemer.

Ruth's acquiescence to her mother-in-law's direction displayed a gentle beauty. In this era of Israel's history, judges led God's people. Horrible things were happening throughout Israel during this time. The book of Judges tells of power struggles, great victories through common people like Gideon and Deborah, and great defeats of mighty men like Samson. The recurring theme throughout Judges is "Everyone did what was right in his own eyes" (17:6 NKJV).

God had set the Israelites apart to be his "peculiar treasure" (Exodus 19:5 KJV). He had given detailed laws through Moses to guide and protect them so that they might be a beacon of light to all the nations around them. Yet everyone was doing their own thing, making their own rules, adjusting God's laws to fit their own preferences.

Boaz had already shown his allegiance to Jehovah and his laws by allowing widows to glean in his fields. Boaz didn't send Ruth away but rather instructed his men to pull a little extra grain from their sheaths and leave some of the best of the firstfruits behind to make it easy for Ruth to gather plenty.

With Boaz showing Ruth such loving-kindness, her acquiescence to Naomi's plan displays an added loveliness. All around them, everyone was doing what was right in their own eyes. In the land Ruth and Naomi had just come from, equal wickedness abounded. Yet here were two "peculiar" people who were set apart by their actions—Boaz by extending grace upon grace to the young widow, and Ruth by acquiescing to her mother-in-law's plan.

When even one person does what is right in God's eyes, the blessing he pours out is so expansive it covers many others for generations to come. The reverse is true as well. One person's destructive choices can bring pain to many for subsequent generations.

Ruth followed Naomi's instructions to the letter. She bathed, perfumed herself, put on her best clothes, and went out to the threshing floor that night. While Boaz was celebrating the gathering of the harvest with the other men, Ruth took note of where he had gone to lie down for the night at the far end of a grain pile. She quietly slipped in, and as Naomi had instructed, Ruth uncovered Boaz's feet and lay beside them waiting.

I wonder what she must have been thinking as she waited, staring at all the stars above Bethlehem that night. Could she possibly imagine that many years in the future, a few shepherds would be tending their flocks under those same stars, and suddenly a host of angels would appear? And the reason for their celestial announcement would be a direct result of this moment of Ruth's willing vulnerability.

But I'm getting ahead of myself.

Back on the threshing floor, sometime in the middle of the night, Boaz awoke, probably because his feet were cold. He realized someone was there and asked, "Who are you?"

"I am your servant Ruth," she answered. "Spread the corner of your garment over me, since you are a [kinsman]-redeemer of our family" (Ruth 3:9).

Here is the picture of covering and protection once again. Whenever I read a place in Scripture where it talks about God drawing us under his wings, I see this scene in which Ruth, in submission to her mother-in-law, came to Boaz and made her request known.

He took her in and assured her, saying, "You have not run after the younger men, whether rich or poor. And now, my daughter, don't be afraid. I will do for you all you ask" (verses 10–11).

And he did. Boaz kept his promise, just as our Kinsman-Redeemer, Jesus Christ, has taken us in, covered us with his unfailing kindness and grace, and keeps his promises to us.

Boaz followed the proper steps, and the deal was struck, so to speak. The elders at the gate who presided over this transaction gave their blessing, saying, "May the LORD make the woman who is coming into your home like Rachel and Leah, who together built up the family of Israel" (4:11).

Boaz took Ruth in as his wife, and "the LORD enabled her to conceive, and she gave birth to a son" (verse 13).

Those who had watched this love story unfold gave their blessing to the new baby boy and reminded Naomi of what God had done. They also gave a telling tribute to Ruth: "For your daughter-in-law, who loves you and is better to you than seven sons, has given him birth" (verse 15).

The story could have ended right there, and we would all be able to pull some instruction, encouragement, and admonition from it. What would it take for people to observe my life and say that I'm obviously a woman who loves my mother-in-law? How willing am I when it comes to giving up what is familiar and comfortable so that I can walk alongside others in their dark season? Especially when I might be in a world of hurt at the same time.

But here is the beautiful extravagance of God's grace in this story: Ruth's baby boy became the father of Jesse, who became the father of David. Yes, David. As in King David, who was in the lineage of Christ. The full line up of all the generations is listed in Matthew, chapter 1.

Ruth, a foreigner who renounced her false gods and put her faith in the God of Israel, was grafted into the royal line of Christ.

The next time we read of another young woman having a baby in Bethlehem, it's Mary. She and her husband, Joseph, made the journey to this tiny town to comply with the census, because they were "of the house and lineage of David" (Luke 2:4 NKJV) and were ancestors of Ruth and Boaz.

What a wild expression of God's loving-kindness to his people. He keeps all his promises. He orchestrates a Grand Story. He never stops loving and providing for us.

I am so glad that Ruth didn't give up and go back to Moab. I am so glad she dared to dream again. Her story flitted through my thoughts as my husband and I prepared for our trek to the faraway land of Brazil.

Chapter 10

HI. GOD LIKES YOU A LOT!

He has made everything beautiful in its time.
He has also set eternity in the human heart; yet no one
can fathom what God has done from beginning to end.

—ECCLESIASTES 3:11

My husband and I had plane tickets in hand and were all set to take off for Brazil. The publisher who had translated the Christy Miller and Sierra Jensen books into Portuguese had arranged a speaking and book-signing tour following the LittWorld conference. During our two-week visit, I was scheduled to speak eleven times in four cities.

Everything was in place when I suddenly developed a toothache. The dentist sent me to the endodontist, who discovered that the cause of the searing pain was a root canal that had gone ballistic. The side of my face swelled, an infection settled into my sinuses, the antibiotic was too strong and made me ill, the painkiller caused my blood pressure to skyrocket, and there I was, back in the hospital again, trying to get my assaulted system to stabilize enough for the endodontist to get back in there and redo the root canal.

Without modern medicine, I think I would have been a goner. All this came at me six days before our flight to Brazil. Logic told me to cancel. My longtime prayer pals, Carrie and Cindy, told me this had all the markings of a spiritual attack. They prayed for God's covering over me, and for his faithful hand to heal me.

During these miserable days, my husband cared for me and prayed for me. He drove me to the endodontist four times in three days and had to walk me to the dentist chair because all the strength had left my body. After two intense dental procedures that included stitches in my gums and a third attempt to prescribe an antibiotic that I didn't react to, the endodontist sent me home to sleep and told me to come back on Thursday morning at 7:30. Our flight to Rio de Janeiro was scheduled to depart at 11:45 that same morning. Would we make the flight? Would I be able to keep my promise to speak so many times over the next two weeks when at the moment I couldn't even walk upstairs by myself?

All I could do was rest, drink lots of fluids, and wait.

The day of our flight arrived and with a last-minute okay from the endodontist, I threw a bunch of clothes into a way-too-big suitcase, and my husband and I dashed to the Portland airport just in time to catch the first of three flights that brought us to Rio. I slept the whole way on every flight and arrived with my face still swollen. I felt as if I was walking in a dreamy slow motion.

"Who's picking us up?" my husband asked as we headed for baggage claim at the Rio de Janeiro airport.

I fumbled with the folded papers in my shoulder bag but couldn't find the schedule from the Brazilian publisher. We were standing in a sea of people with no command of the Portuguese language, and my answer was, "I have no idea."

We decided just to keep walking nice and slow out of baggage claim toward the parking lot. Maybe someone would recognize me from the photo on my website and flag us down. Our plan worked. A friendly man waved us down and greeted us in halting English. All we knew was that we were to follow him. We forced our oversized luggage into his small car and drove into town with him talking enthusiastically in Portuguese and us exchanging bewildered looks.

Our first stop was at a parking lot where an American missionary hopped into the backseat with me. She translated for the driver, telling us that we were in the care of the Christian bookstore's owner, and he was eager for us to see the beaches at Copacabana and Ipanema. Then we would go see the Christ statue.

We had only been on the busy highway a few minutes when another car swerved and collided with the passenger side of our car. We were stunned, but no one was hurt. Our driver pulled to the side of the road, and the translator told me to brace myself, explaining that she had been in two accidents in Brazil in which the car was rear-ended after the initial accident because the shoulder of the road wasn't sufficient to pull the cars all the way out of the traffic.

As we braced ourselves, dozens of cars zoomed past. The driver who had hit us had pulled to the side of the road ahead of us. He got out. Our driver got out. We watched the most unexpected exchange. Both of them smiled, shook hands, examined the damage on each car, and then lifted their hands in the air, gave each other a brief manly sort of hug, and then the guy in the other car drove away.

Our driver got back into the car and then pulled back into the flow of frenetic traffic in jack-rabbit fashion.

"Did the two men know each other?" I asked the translator.

"No. That's just how they do things here. Apparently they decided the damage on the other guy's car was about as bad as the damage on this car, so they called it even and shook on it. Something like this shouldn't put a damper on your day."

I couldn't believe it. What a gracious way to handle an accident.

Nobody yelling or threatening to sue the other person for damages. That's when I realized I wasn't in America.

When we arrived at the Christ statue and headed to the top of the mountain, I looked up in one of the trees and saw a monkey looking down at me. That's when I *really* knew I wasn't in America anymore.

Over the next eight days, my health improved immensely. I was able to speak at every scheduled event and teach all my workshops at the LittWorld conference. When I delivered the keynote address on the final day at LittWorld, a young Brazilian shared the podium with me. Ana Carolina told how the Christy Miller books had affected her life and how God had used the stories to draw her closer to his heart. Ana's presentation was perfect. It was one thing for me to say that novels could change readers' lives around the world, but it was something else entirely when a young woman shared how her own life had been changed.

Christian publishers from around the world heard firsthand how God could use fiction to change lives. Lively discussions sprang up around the table at dinner that evening as writers and publishers from places like the Middle East, Mexico, the Philippines, and India considered the possibility of reaching teens in their countries, in their heart languages, through novels.

A group of us gathered after the evening meal to take the discussion even further. How could writers from difficult places in the world receive this sort of training? How could MAI continue to encourage regional authors to write and publish books in the heart languages of their people? Small seeds were planted that day. We prayed that a beautiful tree of indigenous stories would grow and bear much fruit as they reached young people in the vast corners of the world.

That night, as my husband and I walked back to our room at the conference center, we looked up at the night sky filled with more stars than we could count. These were southern-hemisphere stars. We didn't recognize the constellations, but we whispered to each other the story of Abraham and how God had promised Abraham that he would be the father of a great nation. His offspring would be more numerous than these very stars that dotted the heavens, just as they had when God told Abraham to look up and try to count them.

God had kept his promise to Abraham. I believed he could do anything. He could make the seeds we had planted in the conversations that day grow. He could send millions of books to people all around the world—books written by indigenous authors that told the people of their culture about God's kindness and love. I was thrilled to have a front-row seat to watch God accomplish his purposes as he was about to write another chapter in his Great Story for this generation.

I could hardly sleep that night as I realized that the dreams God had planted in my heart so long ago were coming true in ways I never imagined and in proportions much larger than I had ever fathomed. It was as if I had wished upon a single star when I was twelve that I would become a missionary and travel around the world telling people about God's love. But instead of granting that single-star wish, God lit up the night sky with a thousand wishes, prayers, and dreams come true.

My dream had been very small. God's plan was enormous.

During the remainder of our time in Brazil, we flew to four different cities. Both my husband and I spoke at schools and churches and in an auditorium filled with teenagers. On the last day of our trip, we visited a school where all the girls had read my books as curriculum. The teachers had prepared questions, and the girls were tested on what they read. As we walked into the cafeteria where three hundred teenage Brazilian girls were waiting, they greeted us with a wave of screams as if my husband and I were the real Christy and Todd all grown up and visiting them in Brazil.

To quiet down the girls, I told the translator to invite them to ask questions. One of the girls raised her hand and popped up from her seat. In Portuguese she asked me what she and her friends should do, since the boys in Brazil weren't reading my books.

"What do you mean?" I asked.

She spoke passionately as the translator beside me explained, "She says that after reading your books, she and her friends are making good decisions. They've given their lives to Christ and now want to stay pure and save themselves for their future husbands. But, you see, the boys of Brazil aren't reading these books. They aren't making these same decisions. She wants to know what can be done about that."

My heart pounded in my throat. Every face in that cafeteria was fixed on me, waiting for an answer. This young woman had just identified a global problem for this generation of Christian women. I had heard this frustration voiced many times in letters and emails I received from readers. But no one had ever asked me what could be done about this dilemma of an unbalanced ratio between God-honoring young women and their male contemporaries who were slow to seek God. What could I tell her?

The words I spoke came from my heart: "You can start praying for your future husbands now."

The translator gave her my answer, and a reverent hush came over the room. I caught a brief glimpse of the battle that was going on at that moment for the souls of this generation of young men. Before me was a troop of untrained young women willing to enter that warzone to fight for those men. But how?

Four years later my friend Tricia Goyer and I wrote a book titled *Praying for Your Future Husband* as a direct response to this and several other moments when she and I saw the need for this sort of book for young women.

As we worked on the book, Tricia processed a lot of pieces from her past when she was an unwed teenage mother. We talked about all the miraculous ways God had worked in her life and what redemption looked like twenty years after her first son was born. Tricia was definitely a victim of grace.

A Kindred Victim of Grace

Another teenage girl, a kindred victim of grace who lived thousands of years earlier, had also gotten pregnant before she was married. She had royal blood in her veins, and yet she lived in humble circumstances. God graced this young woman in a most singular way. He called her "highly favored" and did something for her that only happened a few times in the Bible: he sent an angel to give this young woman his message. This hadn't happened to a woman since the time of the judges! God sent the angel Gabriel to visit this teenager, whose name was Mary. He was about to keep his biggest promise of all. The turning point in his Great Story was about to happen. God was sending his Son to be the Savior of the world. And the Lord was going to accomplish his purpose through a young woman.

This reminds me of when I was twenty and traveled with three other college-age women to smuggle Bibles behind the Iron Curtain. The men who worked with the mission couldn't make the trip into what was then Czechoslovakia. The border guards were suspicious of them. But they weren't suspicious of a bunch of young women.

In the same way my girlfriends and I were unsuspected transporters of God's Word into dark places, Mary, our fellow victim of grace, was the unsuspected transporter of God's Son into a dark world.

Like Rebekah, when Mary woke up one morning, everything was as it had always been. But by the time she put her head on her pillow that night, everything had changed.

Gabriel has a lot of mind-bending information for Mary. First, he greets her using a common term of the day: *Shalom*. In Latin his greeting is translated "Ave." The word *shalom* appears in most English translations as "Greetings," although it might be more common for us to say "Hi" or "Hey there" or "Hello."

Can you imagine going about your day and then turning around to see an angel? The angel says to you, "Hey there." And before you can start to breathe again, he tells you that you are "highly favored" and that "the Lord is with you" (Luke 1:28).

Mary was shaken. Quite understandably. How could she not be? Every time angels appeared in Scripture, the first thing they said was "Fear not." At least Gabriel was able to convey the beautiful affirmations to Mary before she showed any confusion or trembled with fear.

The next part of Gabriel's message started with the anticipated line, "Do not be afraid," followed once again by the affirmation, "You have found favor with God" (verse 30). Simplified, this greeting was akin to Gabriel saying, "Hi. God likes you a lot!" Then he told her the most startling piece of news. She was going to have a son! He would be called "the Son of the Most High," and God would "give him the throne of his father David" (verse 32).

This was over the top. More than four hundred years had passed since a prophet had given a message to God's people. And now God had sent Gabriel to reveal the details of God's great plan. And this secret information was given to a young woman!

Mary's response reflected her tender heart. She asked Gabriel, "How will this be?" (verse 34).

Did you catch the key word? She used "will," not "can," in her question. Do you see the evidence of her keen faith in God right there? If she had asked, "How can this be?" it would have indicated skepticism. Instead she simply asked for direction. It's as if she was saying, "What's next?" or "What should I expect?"

Gabriel gave Mary a straightforward answer that was nonetheless laced with poetry, grace, and mystery. "The Holy Spirit will come on you, and the power of the Most High will overshadow you" (verse 35).

The image is similar to what Ruth experienced when she went to Boaz and asked him to cover her. By doing so, Boaz took her in and provided her with a home, protection, and loving-kindness. In the spiritual realm, God was covering Mary with the Holy Spirit, taking her under his wings. His power made the impossible possible in the physical realm. God caused the young virgin to conceive.

In case Mary had any further questions, Gabriel told her that her relative Elizabeth was also with child, even though she was past child-bearing years. Gabriel summed up this stunning bit of news by giving Mary one more affirmation: "For nothing is impossible with God" (verse 37 NLT).

I wonder how many times during the next nine months, or the next thirty-three years, Mary repeated that line to herself. "For nothing is impossible with God."

How many times have you allowed yourself to believe that? When it seems there is no way forward in the midst of whatever situation, season, or trial you're in, nothing is impossible with God.

The best part about this story is how Mary responded to all this stunning news. She acquiesced so beautifully. Her lovely willingness and calm obedience had to have started in her heart for it to flow through her demeanor and her words so effortlessly and with such elegance. Mary told Gabriel that she was the "maidservant" of the Lord and said, "Let it be to me according to your word" (verse 38 NKJV).

In the Phillips translation, this verse reads, "'I belong to the Lord, body and soul … Let it happen as you say.' And at this the angel left her."

What a willing heart! What a surrendered spirit! And what a galaxy full of bright, shining consequences would unfurl over the centuries because of Mary's selfless surrender and unswerving love for God. She didn't understand, but she acquiesced.

Have you ever considered what your life might look like in your times of greatest surprise, upset, confusion, and mystery if, from the heart, you simply said as Mary did, "I belong to the Lord, body and soul.… Let it happen as you say"?

Isn't that the way Jesus taught his disciples to pray: "Your kingdom come, your will be done, on earth as it is in heaven" (Matthew 6:10)?

This prayer is a relinquishing of any small, wish-upon-a-star dreams we might be holding on to in tightly clenched fists, and a receiving of our small part in God's big-picture plan. Our little stories are swept up into his Great Story, and he uses them to accomplish his purposes.

He has given us life. We give that life back to him.

That's the ultimate gift exchange.

I love the following poem by Christina Rossetti titled "A Christmas Carol":

A Christmas Carol

Angels and archangels
May have gathered there,
Cherubim and seraphim
Thronged the air,
But only His mother
In her maiden bliss
Worshipped the Beloved
With a kiss.
What can I give Him,
Poor as I am?
If I were a shepherd
I would bring a lamb;
If I were a wise man
I would do my part,
Yet what I can I give Him,
Give my heart.[4]

What Happens When We Show Up?

I love Christina Rossetti's poem so much that I included it in the Christmas novella, *Finding Father Christmas*, a story about each of us finding our part in the grand Christmas pageant God produced in his

4 Christina Georgina Rossetti, *The Poetical Works of Christina Georgina Rossetti* (London: Macmillan, 1904), 217.

Great Story. The idea for the novella took root on a return trip to England with my daughter the summer after the amazing Brazilian trip. We toured a few villages, and I gathered information for the novella. One highlight was our visit to the charming manor of William Morris, an artist and designer who was a contemporary of Christina Rossetti's and worked closely with her brother. I could picture Christina and other women from the Victorian era sashaying around at an afternoon tea party in the gardens. Morris's Red House became the imagined grand manor of the characters in my Christmas novella.

When I finished *Finding Father Christmas,* I ended up writing a sequel, *Engaging Father Christmas,* because I realized I needed to find out what happened next to the characters!

As the scheduled time for writing the second novella approached, my husband and I received an unexpected call from friends who lived on Maui.

"We're going to the mainland for vacation," they said. "Would you like to come and house-sit for us?"

"When?" we asked.

"August."

"When in August?"

"August. All of August. Can you come for that long? We'll leave our car for you at the airport. All we ask is that you water the banana trees while we're gone."

Needless to say, it didn't take any arm twisting on their part to convince us to accept the invitation, and before we knew it, we were on our way to Maui. While there, we joyfully celebrated our thirtieth wedding anniversary in our friends' lovely tropical home with a flourishing garden in the backyard. We weeded in the cool of the morning and watered the banana trees in the cool of the evening. Often, before breakfast, we walked down the hill to the beach and swam in the turquoise-blue waters before the summer sun rose over the volcano Haleakala.

During the afternoon, I balanced my laptop on my shorts-clad legs and typed away as I swayed in a hammock in the shady backyard. Tropical birds serenaded me, and tall glasses of jasmine green tea quenched my thirst as I wrote about the snowy English countryside at Christmas. It was a wonderful stretch for the imagination to write about winter while in such a setting.

During that month on the island, my husband and I talked a lot about the future. We both agreed that we would love to live on Maui someday, and we brainstormed how that might happen. For almost a year we had been considering a significant investment in a commercial real-estate venture. My husband had checked out every angle. We had prayed, discussed, and prayed some more. During our last few days of house-sitting, we agreed to go ahead and take a risky step of putting all our eggs in one basket by investing in the real estate. It would be two years before we would see a return on the investment, and we thought that might be just about the time we would be ready to have enough of a return to buy a Maui condo.

The Hawaiian dream had been in both of us ever since our first visit to the islands on our honeymoon. In every way, we felt this was what the Lord was leading us to do. We signed the papers and drove to the post office near the airport, sending off the thick packet of documents along with our wishes that this would pay off and allow us to return in a few years.

On our last morning on the island, we rose early and did a final round of yard work. Then I dove into all the housework while my husband finished up outside. We wanted to have everything in tip-top shape for our friends, who were returning that evening.

Before packing up my laptop, I took one last look at emails. In my inbox was an email from a reader named Stacey. She said she was writing to me at midnight because she couldn't sleep. She had been intending to write to me for ten years to tell me how God had used the Christy Miller books in her life. For some reason, that night was when she finally communicated with me.

I stood at the kitchen counter and read the most endearing letter of how, as a young girl, she had been afraid to go to bed because she feared dying. Her mother gave her the first Christy Miller book for Christmas when she was twelve years old. As Stacey read the book in the living room of her family's farm house in rural Canada, she understood that God wanted her to be one of his children, and that to begin such a relationship with him, she needed to give her heart to Jesus. And so she did.

That night she wasn't afraid when she went to bed. She knew that Jesus was with her.

Stacey's letter went on to explain how she started asking God for "just one thing." First it was for Christian friends, like the friends Todd and Christy had in the books. God answered her prayer, and her Christian friends invited her to go to church with them, which she did.

Then, in high school, Stacey asked God for "just one thing": to go to a Christian college. Miraculously, it happened.

As college was winding up, she asked for "just one thing." This time her request was that one day she could go to Maui, the way Todd and Christy did in the stories. She sent off applications for internship programs in children's ministry, and the church that took her on was Hope Chapel in Kihei, Maui.

By this point in reading Stacey's email, my jaw went slack. The friends we were house-sitting for attended Hope Chapel. Their house was only a few miles from the church, and that was where we had gone each Sunday. I wondered whether Stacey was still an intern at Hope and had been there the past four Sundays.

I kept reading the email and discovered that when her two-year internship program ended, she had asked God for "just one thing": that she would find a job on Maui so that she could stay longer. A position for a preschool teacher opened up in the nearby town of Kahului, and she was offered the job. That was where she worked now, the email said, and what she loved most about her job was that every day she could tell little children that they didn't have to be afraid, because Jesus was always with them. He always heard their prayers and promised to answer them.

The end of Stacey's email summarized her reason for writing to me in the middle of the night. She said she had recently asked God for "just one thing"—that she could meet me one day and say thank you face-to-face for writing the Christy Miller books. If I had given up writing the stories, she didn't know how she would ever have come to know Jesus as she did, and she would have been living a very different life.

I was weeping by this point. Her final paragraph said that since she didn't even know where I lived, and since it really was impossible that the two of us would ever cross paths on this earth, she believed this would be the "just one thing" she would ask of God that he wouldn't answer. That's why she needed to write the long email to tell me her story, since she knew we wouldn't meet till heaven.

My hands were shaking as I walked out to the front yard and motioned for my husband to stop the lawn mower. I tearfully told him everything Stacey had written.

My husband had only one thing to say: "Get in the car."

"Why?"

"She said she worked at the preschool. I know right where that is. It's not far from the car wash. I'll drop you off, you can go say hi, and I'll get the car washed. Come on, we don't have a lot of time."

"But I need a shower." I looked down at my dirty T-shirt and baggy shorts.

He wasn't listening. He already was heading for the garage to put away the lawn mower. Jiggling the car keys, he motioned for me to step it up and get in the car.

I acquiesced.

We drove the seven miles into town with me fidgeting all the way. I didn't know what I would say or how it would look for me to barge into her classroom. That is, if I could figure out which classroom was hers without disrupting the whole preschool. I only knew her first name.

Still, it was pretty incredible that the Lord had kept her awake the night before and put it on her heart to type those words only twelve hours ago, when, of course, she had no idea I was on Maui and would be boarding a plane in a few hours to fly back to Portland.

He is the God who made the world. He also made everything in it. He is the Lord of heaven and earth. He doesn't live in temples built by hands. He is not served by human hands. He doesn't need anything. He himself gives life and breath to all people. He also gives them everything else they have. From one man he made all the people of the world. Now they live all over the earth. He decided exactly when they should live. And he decided exactly where they should live. God did this so that people would seek him. Then perhaps they would reach out for him and find him. They would find him even though he is not far from any of us. "In him we live and move and exist." As some of your own poets have also said, "We are his children."

—Acts 17:24–28 NIrV

We pulled into the school parking lot, and I chickened out. "I feel ridiculous," I told my husband.

"So?"

"I look so messy, and I smell awful."

"So?" My husband had no sympathy.

My hand clutched the car door handle. "Will you wait here? Just wait. I'll be real quick, and then I'll go to the car wash with you. If she's not here, I don't want to be loitering, waiting for you to come back."

"Okay, I'll wait. Go."

I clambered out of the car, walked down the quiet corridor, and felt the welcoming trade winds airing out my sweaty T-shirt. It was nap time, and through the classrooms' open doors, I could see the little children stretched out on their nap mats. A woman was standing at the end of the hallway posting a list of some sort on a bulletin board. I went up to her and quietly asked, "Can you tell me which room is Stacey's?"

"It's that one." She pointed to the

door that had a grass hula skirt tacked to the top of the door frame and a sign over the door that read, "Welcome to the Beach." I saw a young woman inside sitting in a rocking chair, and I motioned for her to come to the door. I had no idea what Stacey looked like.

"Are you Stacey?" I asked.

"No, she's in the teachers' lounge. That way. At the end of the hall."

"Thank you." I tried to keep my flip-flops from flopping too loudly as I headed toward the lounge.

When I was about halfway down the hall, the lounge door opened, and a young woman walked out. She walked about five steps, looked up, saw me coming toward her, and then froze. Stacey had seen my photo on my website the night before when she went there to get my email address. I could tell that she recognized me. I could also tell that she was stunned.

Not knowing what else to say or do, I walked up to her and said, "Hi. I got your email!"

Poor Stacey! I can't image what it would be like to write an email to someone you've never met, to pour out your heart and say, "I'll meet you in heaven!" and then, twelve hours later, to look up and find that person in your face.

In a tiny way, it must have been the way Mary felt when Gabriel just showed up and said, "Hi. God likes you a lot."

But of course, I neither looked nor smelled anything like an angelic being.

Stacey started crying. And shaking. I was already shaking, so I joined in with the crying. Then we hugged and giggled like the children who were watching us through the open door of a nearby classroom.

"How?" Stacey said when her words finally managed to cooperate. Her poor brain was trying to piece together the possibility of someone receiving an email, jumping on a private jet, and then flying across the Pacific Ocean to show up at the preschool where she worked.

I gave her an abbreviated version of why we were on the island and how my husband had made me track her down before we left for the mainland.

Stacey and I laughed again and wiped away more tears of wonder. Then I asked her if I could bless her. She nodded. I placed my hand on her forehead and said, "Stacey, may the Lord bless you and keep you. May the Lord make his face to shine upon you and give you his peace. And may you always love Jesus first, above all else."

We cried some more, and in an airy whisper, she said, "I guess nothing is impossible for God."

As we flew back to Portland that evening, we headed into the east, where the day had already closed its eyes and night had come. I looked out the window of the plane and saw a big ole Maui moon held in place in the inky sky by invisible hands. All of that amazing moonlight was reflected. None of the luminescence was generated from the moon itself. The moon is dust. I am dust. Dry bones and dust.

> I believe that each work of art, whether it is a work of great genius or something very small, comes to the artist and says, "Here I am. Enflesh me. Give birth to me." And the artist either says, "My soul doth magnify the Lord," and willingly becomes the bearer of the work, or refuses; but the obedient response is not necessarily a conscious one.
>
> —*Madeleine L'Engle, Walking on Water*

Yet, when my heart is turned fully to the Son, he reflects his glory all over me, and I can light up the darkness.

I know these are elemental thoughts. But that's why I liked them so much on that return trip from a month on Maui. "The kingdom of heaven belongs to such as these," Jesus said about the children who gathered around him (Matthew 19:14). Elemental trust and understanding, childlike faith and wonder—these were the souvenirs I was bringing back with me. Loving God was a lot less complicated than I had made it over the years. God still had plans for me. He was ready to take my breath away and startle me all over again.

And I was ready and oh so willing to acquiesce. Like Mary, I was looking into the future and asking, "How will this be?" I was listening for the echo from the courts of heaven that said, "Nothing is impossible with God."

Chapter 11

GOING HOME

They were glad when it grew calm,
and he guided them to their desired haven.
Let them give thanks to the Lord *for his unfailing love*
and his wonderful deeds for mankind.

— Psalm 107:30 – 31

The following year our son was married on a gorgeous Saturday in February.

A few months later our daughter completed her second year of college.

My husband continued to see lives changed through his counseling ministry as many men broke free from cycles of addiction.

I kept on writing, writing, writing. Opportunities opened up for me to speak at several events around the country for women and teens.

Life was good. We were in a sunny summertime season of our days. The spray of every sprinkler revealed a rainbow of blessings. Every cherry ripened nice and sweet on the tree. Our home was a haven for a wonderful circle of people. Friends and family gathered for holidays.

Thanksgiving was my favorite. My husband's favorite holiday was the Fourth of July. All was well.

Except for one thing. The economy was dipping. Like an ominous cloud that loomed on the horizon, the investment we had put all our resources into cast a darkness over all our hopes for the future. We prayed, waited, and evaluated our situation and then prayed some more. We continued to give generously, and my husband and I resorted to nail biting only in front of each other behind closed doors. Some days it seemed that everything was going to be A-OK, but other days we pictured ourselves on the other side of the lunch line at the soup kitchen.

Two years passed, and the LittWorld conference rolled around once again. This time the conference was to be held in Africa. When I was invited to teach, my heart did a jig. At last! At long last! I was going to Africa. And not just Africa. I was going to Nairobi, Kenya. The conference center where we would stay, in the highlands among the verdant rolling tea fields, was in the same area I had applied for the laundry-supervisor position so long ago.

Ever since the first LittWorld conference I attended in England, where I had met Wambura, she and I had kept in touch. I called to let her know I was coming to her hometown, and she, too, remembered the laundry-supervisor position.

"You must stay with me after the conference," she said.

"I'd love to."

"I will take you to meet my parents, and we will go up Mount Kenya and see the elephants and the zebras."

"I can't wait!"

"And there is one more thing you must do when you come to stay at my house."

"Sure, what is it?" I asked.

"I have decided that I want to participate in God's will for your life, so I will let you wash my laundry."

I laughed and told her she needed to get a big basket so I could put it on my head and carry the laundry down to a river somewhere.

Now she was the one laughing, because she lived in a modern apartment building in downtown Nairobi. It would be quite a trek to find a river.

On the long flight to Nairobi, I reveled in the privilege of once again being with writers and publishers from around the world. During the conference, we bent our heads over cups of steaming Kenyan chai and discussed how to get more books with the good news of Jesus into more hands. As a group we traveled by bus and spent the afternoon at Lake Naivasha in the Rift Valley, where we saw hippos wiggle their ears and zebras scatter through the acacia trees. At a wildlife preserve, I fed a giraffe out of the palm of my hand, and in the town of Karen, we saw the house that was used in the film *Out of Africa*.

And we danced. Oh yes we did. We danced with our faces radiant like the moon.

When the conference ended, I went with Wambura on a beautiful journey up Mount Kenya, just as she had promised. We spent the night at a hotel built in the treetops, with windows all around. From the upper deck, we were served tea in proper china teacups as we gazed down on the jungle. Directly below was a large watering hole where the wild beasts gathered after sunset. Wambura and I made ourselves comfy, just a couple of Sisterchicks having tea with the elephants, as if we did such things every evening at twilight.

On our way back to Wambura's home, we crossed a river in a rural area. Along the riverside four young women were washing clothes.

The scene was so tranquil. The grass along the riverside was the deep, luscious shade of emeralds. The river, flowing from the skirts of Mount Kenya, glistened in the afternoon sunshine. A darling baby sat contentedly beside his mother as she plunged a light blue sweater into a bucket of water she had carried up from the river.

"Stop the car! Please, I have to get out," I said to Wambura. My heart was pounding wildly.

Wambura understood. This was my river. She asked where my camera was and said, "Go. You have waited a long time to get your hands on some African laundry. Introduce yourself to her first. It will be fine."

I got out, looking ever so American in my jeans and turquoise embroidered shirt. I was still twenty-two years old in my heart as I strode toward the women, smiling with my perfectly straight teeth and my naïveté showing all over my face.

"*Jambo*," I greeted the women. I only knew a few words in Swahili, but I also knew it was likely that the women spoke English like most Kenyans.

The small gathering of laundresses stared at me. Even the baby stared. I felt so white. So awkward.

Addressing the woman I had seen washing the sweater, I said, "My name is Robin, and I'm not sure I can really explain why, but may I put my hands in your bucket? I need to wash some clothes in Africa before I die. May I? Please?"

The woman blinked, looked at the other women, and then cautiously nodded.

I plunged my hands into that bucket of cold water and took hold of that pale-blue sweater as if this were my final act of service on earth. The tears fell from my eyes and mingled with the luminous soap bubbles. It was happening. I was in Africa. In Kenya. And I was washing clothes at a river, in the sunlight. Village women were beside me. There was even a baby who had fixed his big brown eyes on mine.

An ancient whisper echoed in my heart. *You didn't make this up. When you told this story to the girls in your Sunday school class long ago, I had already written this moment into your life. Before you were born, I knew you. I am the one who planted this story in you. This is part of my Great Story. I planted every dream you hold in your heart. I am accomplishing my purposes for you, Robin. Trust me.*

Still crying a reservoir full of swift, silent tears, I drew my hands up out of their clarifying baptism and forced my voice to say thank you to my gentle hostess. "God bless you," I added.

Her smile spread wide. "And God bless you, *rafiki*."

Rafiki. Friend. That was one of the Swahili words I knew.

I leaned over and kissed the top of her baby's head, feeling the soft, natty curls on my lips. With quick steps I trotted back to the car, where Wambura waited, camera in hand.

We got back on the bumpy road without exchanging words. I dried my eyes, drew in a deep breath, and fixed my gaze on the enormous puffs of white clouds that sailed effortlessly through the brilliant blue sky.

"Well?" Wambura asked after the tingles of the moment had calmed themselves on the back of my neck. "What do you think?"

"That was ..." I didn't know how to describe what the completion of that circle meant. "It was ..."

She glanced at me and grinned. "It was not what you were created to do, was it?"

"No, it wasn't. I can say with full assurance that being a laundry supervisor was not God's will for my life." I smiled back at her.

We ambled on down the rutted road for a stretch, and all I could think was how passionately I wished that every woman could put her hands into the bucket of her unanswered prayers. What a powerful thing it was to hear the affirming echo in my heart that God's ways are perfect. He has plans for us that are bigger than any dream or whim we could ever wish for ourselves.

Now the power that has planned this experience for us is God, and he has given us his Spirit as a guarantee of its truth. This makes us confident, whatever happens.

—2 Corinthians 5:5 PHILLIPS

As I was lost in the wonder, Wambura gave me a nudge. "You should know that what just happened here does not excuse you from washing my laundry when we get to my house. I have the big basket all ready."

She really did.

Once again we took pictures. My favorite shot is of the two of us standing in the hallway at Wambura's apartment. I was balancing a big woven basket on my head, and both of us were laughing from a place deep inside, a place of friendship, womanhood, and the joy of realizing we were together inside an eternal moment. Wambura and I are Sisterchicks forever! This, too, was a dream not crafted by human efforts. Every woman should know such a kindred spirit, such a *rafiki*, such a kindred victim of grace.

I flew home via Amsterdam and stayed with my *rafiki* Anne, another one of my Sisterchicks. She and I had met in Germany at the Frankfurt Book Fair and then shared a room at my first LittWorld Conference when she'd been battling the effects of malaria from a trip to a remote corner of Africa. She met me at the Amsterdam airport on my return flight from Nairobi and I couldn't speak. The slow, silent tears wound their way down my cheeks. Anne, who has seen many sides to the mysterious continent, looked at me with compassion. "Oh, my friend, what did Africa do to you?"

I didn't know how to say that Africa had fixed me when I didn't even know I was broken. But I didn't need to say anything. Anne understood, just as she had understood so many other barely spoken thoughts during our midlife stretch of years. She was my soul-twin during a season of life when both of us were discovering that God delighted in giving his daughters unexpected gifts at unexpected times. It was in the shade of her hospitality that I began to process how close God had seemed while I was in Africa.

On the long flight back to Portland a few days later, I thought about what it's like to be so rich when you're more than half a century old. Our family's savings account had been emptied, and we weren't sure we could keep our home. But I felt so very rich—rich in friends, rich in family, rich in love and in all the Lord's lavish blessings.

I felt very full when I arrived home, strode past airport security, and tumbled into my husband's arms. The deepened lines in his forehead told me what had happened on American soil while I was away. Our investment had indeed failed. All the money we had put into the project two years earlier was lost.

For the next year, we both worked as hard as we could. And we prayed even harder. We talked for many hours about what to do and where to live. Every prayer was answered with silence. We felt so foolish. We shouldn't have put all our eggs in one basket. We shouldn't have taken such a risk. We looked each other in the eye and said with clear hearts that at the time we made the decision to enter the investment, we did it as a team. Both of us thought that was how God was leading.

Does God give and take away? Yes. We knew he did. If he wanted to take away our house, that was okay. It was his to take. It had always been his house, even from that day years earlier when our Realtor first took our nine-year-old daughter up to her bedroom and told her a gazebo would be built in view of her window. We knew then that God had hand selected this as the place we were supposed to live. Now we were about to put a For Sale sign in the yard, with no idea where we would go next.

The LORD *your God is testing you to find out whether you love him with all your heart and with all your soul. It is the* LORD *your God you must follow, and him you must revere. Keep his commands and obey him; serve him and hold fast to him.*

—Deuteronomy 13:3–4

While we floated in a fog of uncertainty, I privately mourned the loss of our house. In January I sat in my snuggle chair by the window and read through my journal from the previous year. Tears fell on the pages as I opened my hand and asked the Lord for a new word. In his extravagance he gave me more than just one word. The phrase that pressed up against the windowpanes of my soul was "Steady on; stay the course."

I had no idea what that meant.

At Easter we filled the house with every relative we could find within a thousand-mile radius. A cousin I hadn't seen in forty years found out about the gathering and joined us with his wife and daughters. I told him about the healing moment of forgiveness that had happened between my dad and our uncle. I took a picture of him beside my brother. They hadn't seen each other since my brother was seven years old. Our son and his wife kept the collection of little second cousins entertained while my niece and our "adopted" son and his wife helped me keep food coming from the kitchen. A lot of huge stones were rolled away that day. We were well positioned to see the Lord's resurrection power displayed in our lives.

On the Fourth of July, my husband and I hosted the biggest bash yet, with every friend, neighbor, and their dogs that we could fit in beach chairs in the driveway. Oohs, aahs, and barks abounded as we watched the spectacular fireworks burst into sparkling colors and fall like evaporating confetti over the gazebo in the park across the street.

For our present troubles are small and won't last very long. Yet they produce for us a glory that vastly outweighs them and will last forever!

—2 Corinthians 4:17 NLT

Then Thanksgiving Day arrived, my favorite holiday. My husband and I were all alone as we ran tape guns over the tops of dozens of packed boxes. In the morning the movers would arrive, and we would hand over the keys to the blessed front door of the dear old friend and treasured dwelling place we had called home for so many years.

A Kindred Victim of Grace

A woman stepped out of the pages of history to encourage me during that long year of wondering, watching, and waiting, of holding on to the phrase God had given me—"Steady on; stay the course." She was a woman who also knew that disaster was coming and that in the tumble, she would lose her home, and much more.

This woman was a wife and a mother. She had three sons, all of whom were married. Her husband stood out among all the men at that time. Why? He did what was right in the Lord's sight. Have you guessed who he is? He lived almost six thousand years ago, and his name is still recognized throughout the world. If you grew up going to Sunday school, you probably knew about him before you ever heard of Adam, Abraham, or Jacob. You probably even sang a little song about him that ends with these two lines:

Noah found grace in the eyes of the Lord
And he landed high and dry.

Despite all of Noah's fame, his wife's name is never mentioned. She is referred to only as "Noah's wife."

So why was I suddenly relating to her so intimately as all the leaves were falling off the trees and I headed into another autumn of my days? Because she lost everything. Everything but her husband, her sons, and her daughters-in-law. She let all the rest go. Why? Because God had directed her husband to do something that appeared ridiculous to everyone, and yet he did it.

Twice in Genesis we read that Noah did exactly what God commanded him to do (6:22; 7:5). Even though building an enormous ark made no sense and made Noah look insane, he did it.

What did Noah's wife do? Apparently she kept her mouth shut and went along for the ride.

Now that's faith right there.

Noah's wife stands out not because of what she did but because of what she didn't do. She isn't quoted anywhere in the whole amazing story of the flood. Think of the key men whom God used throughout his Great Story, and then think of what is recorded about their wives.

God spoke face-to-face with Moses and called Abraham his friend. He distinguished David as a man with a heart for God. God singled out Job for deliberate testing. These men were all married, and their wives went through everything they went through as kindred victims of grace. Along the way, some rather poignant statements from these wives were recorded for all time:

- Sarai, the wife of Abram: "Go, sleep with my slave; perhaps I can build a family through her" (Genesis 16:2). (We saw how that idea turned out.)
- Rebekah, the wife of Isaac: "Now, my son, listen carefully and do what I tell you" (Genesis 27:8). She proceeded to tell Jacob how to trick his aging father into giving her son the blessing instead of giving it to Esau. When the plan worked and Esau was furious, Rebekah set up another plan to persuade Isaac to send Jacob off to find a wife among her people. Her statement, recorded for posterity was "I'm disgusted with living because of these Hittite women. If Jacob takes a wife from among the women of this land, from Hittite women like these, my life will not be worth living" (verse 46).
- Zipporah, the wife of Moses: "Surely a bloody husband art thou to me" (Exodus 4:25 KJV).
- Job's wife: "Curse God and die!" (Job 2:9).
- Samson's wife: "You hate me! You don't really love me. You've given my people a riddle, but you haven't told me the answer" (Judges 14:16).
- Michal, David's wife: "You are the king of Israel. You have really brought honor to yourself today, haven't you? You have taken off your royal robe right in front of the female slaves of your officials. You acted like someone who is very foolish!" (2 Samuel 6:20 NIrV).

All of these women were married to men whom God had blessed and had used mightily for his kingdom. Each of them had something to say about her husband's behavior when he was doing what he believed God had asked him to do. And what came out of the mouths of these women weren't words of support and affirmation. They made sure their opinions were heard. Not only did their husbands hear what they had to say, but God also heard, and he recorded it word for word.

With Noah's wife, the big surprise is that none of her words were recorded, positive or negative. It doesn't mean she didn't have days when she doubted, grieved, was frightened or furious. It doesn't mean she didn't speak up on those days. It's just that, for whatever reason, God didn't record anything other than the fact that Noah had a wife. And when the moment came for them to board the ark, she did and went along for the ride, even if she didn't understand what God was doing.

We know that the flood lasted forty days and forty nights. We know that the huge ark housed two of every kind of animal and required the nonstop efforts of the eight people on board to feed and clean up after all those creatures every single day. The sounds and smells of that floating zoo must have been unspeakable.

But here's the thing. The rain may have lasted 40 days and nights, but Noah and his family were stuck in the middle of God's mysterious plan on the ark for 376 days. More than a year. A year of floating along in stinky, super-uncomfortable conditions, and all the while, Noah's wife knew that everything she had owned, loved, or enjoyed outside of their immediate family was now gone. Demolished. Taken by the God her husband served without wavering.

And for the hundred years it took Noah to build the ark, as well as more than a year that Noah's family was locked up inside of it, not one word that Noah's wife spoke was recorded. God accomplished his great plan whether they were crazy about it or not.

This is such a vivid picture of how the blessing happens inside the obedience. God said, "Come into the ark" (Genesis 7:1 NKJV), and they did. Then God shut the door and locked them up inside. Outside the storms raged. The world as they had known it was destroyed. For more than a year they wondered what was going to happen next. Where would they live? How would they eat? What would happen when all their resources ran out? All they could do was wait.

When the time was right, God spoke to them again: "Come out of the ark" (8:15). What a long stretch of silence between "Come into the ark" and "Come out of the ark." The exact length of time passed according to God's curious plan. They too heard God's command: "Steady on; stay the course." Oh, it might not have been those exact words, but the concept was the same.

God shows evidence of the perfect timing of his plan in several places in his Great Story.

When Moses led the children of Israel out of Egypt, it was 430 years to the day when they had gone into bondage. When they set foot in the Promised Land after what seemed like a devastating detour through the wilderness, on God's time schedule it was "to the day," according to the events on his calendar. When Mary gave birth to Christ, it was when "the fulness of time [had] come" (Galatians 4:4 KJV).

When Isaiah recorded the prophecies of Israel's restoration, he described it this way: "This is what the LORD says: 'At just the right time, I will respond to you. On the day of salvation I will help you. I will protect you and give you to the people as my covenant with them. Through you I will reestablish the land of Israel and assign it to its own people again' " (Isaiah 49:8 NLT).

Speaking of the Lord's return to earth, Timothy wrote, "At just the right time Christ will be revealed from heaven by the blessed and only almighty God, the King of all kings and Lord of all lords" (1 Timothy 6:15 NLT).

We might think we have things all figured out, and we have a good plan in place for our lives, but always and ultimately we're on God's time schedule. At just the right time, he does what he desires to accomplish his purposes. He does this by breathing on us his grace, his breath of life, his Spirit.

When the time came for the waters of the flood to recede, how was God to accomplish such an impossible task? Genesis 8:1 says, "But God remembered Noah and all the wild animals and the livestock that were with him in the ark, and he sent a wind over the earth, and the waters receded."

What a magnificent image of his Spirit, like a wind, accomplishing his purposes, putting things aright, covering his creation with his endless grace.

Waiting to Hear from God

Before our Thanksgiving packing fest, my husband and I had spent the year stuck inside God's mysterious plan, the way Noah and his family were stuck inside the ark. We were waiting for him to show us what we should do next. Miles away in Southern California, our daughter had also been in a state of waiting and wondering. She had been waiting patiently and with purity for the right guy to come along and was beginning to wonder if he ever would.

Then one ordinary Thursday afternoon, she called and said, "I met this guy ..."

"And?" I prompted.

"He's a youth pastor, like dad was."

"And?"

"I don't know. There's something about him." She told me his full name, and I stopped her midsentence.

"Wait. Do you by any chance know his parents' names?"

"His dad's name is Ray."

I lowered myself into the nearest chair. My heart was pounding. "Honey, is his mom's name Marjie?"

"Yeah, I think it is. Why? Do you know them?"

"Know them!? Marjie was my college roommate."

"No! Really?"

"Yes, really!"

At just the right time, our daughter and her new "almost boyfriend" flew up to Portland for a friend's wedding. The boyfriend asked my husband for permission to pursue a serious relationship with our daughter. Permission was granted heartily. To make the moment especially memorable, the boyfriend asked our daughter if she wanted to go for a walk that evening in the rain.

No, she didn't want to go for a walk in the rain. Rain, rain, so much rain. But he convinced her and led the way across the street. They dashed under the sheltering protection of the gazebo, where he expressed his heartfelt intentions for her and their possible future together. She acquiesced, and the next chapter of their love story began.

We rejoiced with them that night, but the next morning a heavy sadness weighed on us. My husband and I met our Realtor at the title office at nine to sign the papers that relinquished our home to the new buyer. We had stalled our decision to sell for almost a year and a half. We had long talks with our Realtor. She was the one who had sold us the house, and she knew how much love had filled that space, starting with the verses we marked on the floors before the carpets were laid.

When at last we needed to put the house on the market, we had posted the sign in the front yard and joined the dozen other homes in our neighborhood that were for sale. Some of them had been on the market for two years or longer.

Our house sold in three weeks. We can't explain why. God did that. For just the right price at just the right time. And yet, I was having a difficult time seeing that on the morning we picked up pens and placed our names on the lines that indicated "seller."

As we left the office, the Realtor asked about our kids. I found a smile rising as I told her about our daughter and her new boyfriend and what had transpired the night before in the gazebo.

"In the gazebo?" Tears welled in our Realtor's eyes as she repeated, "He took her to the gazebo? Don't you remember? That was your daughter's wish when you moved into the house. I've never forgotten the way she said that she asked God for a gazebo, and he gave it to her."

Now I was teary-eyed.

"This all makes sense to me now," our Realtor said. "This is why you didn't list the house a year and a half ago when we first talked about it. This is how specific God is with his timing. He was waiting until your daughter could have that special moment last night in her gazebo. God planned this for her from the very beginning. I just know it."

I lavish unfailing love for a thousand generations on those who love me and obey my commands.

—Exodus 20:6 NLT

We had sixty days to sort and pack after our house was sold. In the middle of our packing, we took a break and flew to Maui for five days to help with some needed repairs to my father-in-law's vacation condo. My father-in-law had wanted to sell the condo he had used as a vacation rental for the past thirty-four years, but it needed some work before it was put on the market. Our family had spent many happy vacations in that oceanfront unit, and since my husband had been the designated renovator of the unit over the years, we welcomed the chance to escape to the island for a few days.

While we were there, we had dinner with friends we had known since we were in college.

They asked, "Why don't you move here to Maui? You've been talking about it for more than thirty years."

We told them we couldn't afford it. We were looking at condos to rent in Portland. We confessed that we had dreamed about moving to Maui ever since the nine-month sabbatical we had spent in the family condo twenty years earlier, but every time we asked the Lord if we could move back to Maui, he either made it clear the answer was no or he was silent.

"So?" our friend said. "Ask him again."

The next day my husband and I drove to the other side of the island to visit the friends we had house-sat for many summers ago. On the way we argued. The "ask God again" comment from dinner the night before had sprinkled enough dream dust on me that I was asking, "Why not?" My husband was hesitant, saying he didn't want to force the possibility.

Our entire marriage had been a series of mutual choices about where we could best serve the Lord, and all our moves in the past had been based on where the ministry opportunities had opened up for both of us, but primarily for my husband.

"But what if this is where the Lord wants us to serve him next?" I asked.

The sky above us was filled with clouds that resembled a whole flock of fluffy, white sheep grazing in an azure meadow. The ocean to our right shimmered in the sunlight, wearing an unbearably beautiful gown of flowing aquamarine. The air was warm as the trade winds blew through the open car windows like a gentle caress on that October morning. Maui was then and always had been the home of my heart. I needed no further convincing that this was where we could live and move and have our being.

My husband firmly stood on the side of waiting for God to make his plans for us clear.

"What would you need?" I asked. "What would it take to get you to consider moving here? A Macedonian call like the one Paul got in Acts when he dreamed of the guy from Macedonia saying, 'Come over here and help us'? Is that what you'd need?"

"It would be nice. Then at least we'd know that's what God wants, and we're not trying to finagle the decision."

I remembered the example of Noah's wife and chose to do something new and different. I said nothing.

An hour later, through some unexpected circumstances, my husband and I walked into the office of Hope Chapel, the church we'd attended during our previous stay on the island. It was the same church where Stacey had done her internship before taking the position at the preschool in Kahului. I knew that Stacey had returned to her Canadian hometown, because we had stayed in contact. Now, as we entered the church, a new college intern greeted us, looked at me, and then blurted out, "Are you Robin Jones Gunn?"

"Yes."

The girl, whose name was Alyssa, started weeping. "Your books! I've read all your books! It's because of your stories that I'm here. You discipled me with everything you wrote about, and I never would be where I am in my relationship with the Lord today if it weren't for your books."

We hugged, grinned, and laughed. The senior pastor came out of his office to ask what was going on. We introduced ourselves to the pastor and explained that we had attended Hope Chapel years before during our August stay. We hadn't met a lot of people on our previous visits. It surprised us when the pastor graciously invited us to come into his office and chat. We did what the Hawaiians call "talk story" for more than an hour. Then the pastor said, "I feel compelled to pray. Would you two pray with me?"

We bowed our heads and felt the Holy Spirit's presence breathing over us as the first words out of the pastor's mouth were, "Father, would you give the Gunns a Macedonian call? No, make that a Maui call. Tell them to come over here and help us."

My husband and I reached for each other's hands and squeezed tightly. Neither of us had said anything about our earlier conversation in the car on the way over. We had only mentioned that we were in a place where we were open to what the Lord would have us do next.

And there it was, the exact words prayed over us less than two hours after we had squabbled over the question, "What would it take?" As soon as the pastor said "Amen," my husband turned to me and said, "This is it. This is what's next."

That night, on faith, we booked two one-way tickets to Maui for December 14. The airfares jumped significantly on December 15. We didn't know where we would live or how it was going to work out, but we knew God. We knew the way he had led us over the years, and we recognized his fingerprints all over this.

I had a feeling I would have no difficulty following my husband into the "ark" that led us to this place where everything about life as we had known it was now radically altered. We figured out our budget and knew that all we could afford would be a one- or two-bedroom condo. My father-in-law's place wasn't an option because of the impending sale, but we had friends on Maui checking the rental listings for us. Nothing was happening. We had ordered the moving container and agreed to be out of our house the day after Thanksgiving, but we still didn't know where we were going to live. I reminded myself over and over of the year's phrase: Steady on; stay the course.

It wasn't long before God acted on our behalf. A friend from Hope Chapel was doing his weekly mowing at the church when another church member happened to ask if he knew anyone looking to rent a house. He told our friend that he needed someone to move in by December 15!

Our friend called with the news while I was in California speaking at a women's retreat the weekend before Thanksgiving. My talks had been centered on the theme of trusting God and believing in his unfailing kindness, even when you can't see what he is doing.

None of the women there knew the depth of suspense I was in as my husband and I waited on the Lord. In eight days the container packed with our worldly possessions would be placed on a freight ship that would float across the Pacific Ocean and deposit it on the island of

Maui on December 15. We had no idea where to tell the truck driver to deliver the container—until that call came to me at the end of the women's retreat.

We had a house to rent. And not just a house. A house with five bedrooms and a lanai (balcony) where we could sit and watch the whales breech in the ocean less than a mile away. The two-year-old house could rent for far more than we were able to pay, but the owner said he and his wife wanted it to be used for ministry.

Since the moment we moved in, right on schedule on December 15, that beautiful Maui home became a place of ongoing ministry. We offered the extra downstairs bedroom to a young woman who needed a nest, rent-free, for five months. The other downstairs bedroom made the perfect vacation suite for the seventy-eight guests who visited in a steady stream the first year we were here. To my utter delight, one of those guests was Wambura. Full circle. From Kenya to Maui and back.

I continued to write the stories God put on my heart. I continued to speak at local events and also went to Bulgaria to train writers at an MAI workshop. My husband started up a counseling practice and launched a men's group at church. We hosted a weekly *ohana,* home group, and even had a visiting film producer over for dinner one evening to discuss how the Lord might be leading to produce a film or television program based on the Christy Miller books. We had so much to talk about, our dinner lasted a record-breaking nine hours. Together we prayed under a Maui moon with a sky filled with too many stars to count.

Our daughter was married in California last summer—in a gazebo. As we gathered with so many family and friends at the happy reunion and grand celebration of many prayers answered, my college roomie, Marjie, and I put our arms around each other and smiled our biggest happy-mama smiles.

"Did you ever think we would be this blessed?" she asked me.

I had no words. Only tears.

November arrived, and for our first Thanksgiving in the islands, we set up long tables on the grass in the backyard. I covered the tables with my best gold-colored tablecloths, arranged twenty-four place settings with fine china plates, and decorated with candles and vibrant flowers from the tropical bushes all around us—plumerias, red ginger, helaconia, and bird of paradise.

At sunset our friends and family arrived bearing every sort of traditional Thanksgiving food as well as local favorites, such as taro dinner rolls. They're purple on the inside and taste especially delicious with a dab of cranberry relish and a touch of warm gravy.

As a balmy breeze cooled our slices of pumpkin pie, the tiki torches around the backyard flickered. It was a remarkable change from Thanksgivings around the dining-room table in Portland, where we had warmed ourselves by the fireplace and gazed out the window at the amber leaves clinging to the trees.

One tradition was the same. We lingered at the table, and every guest took a turn standing and sharing how God had blessed them over the previous year. The words of praise in that tropical garden were bountiful, and the presence of God's abiding Spirit was as vivid as the concert of piercingly bright stars that covered us with a canopy twinkling with promise.

In every way I knew my husband and I were home. Not necessarily because we had lived on Maui for nearly a year but because we were home where God wanted us to be, and both of us were carrying out the work we were created to do. God's kingdom was coming into our lives there in the backyard as we gathered with his people, remembered his goodness, and sang his praise. That's what made the lovely rental house "home." His presence and his children gathered in one place. That's what will one day make heaven "Home," with a capital *H*.

A few weeks ago, a new friend, Marlene, brought over a book and said, "This made me think of you when I was reading it. Have you ever heard of Corrie ten Boom?"

That evening I opened the book to a section where Corrie was writing about the rental house she had moved into in Placentia, California, in 1977. The similarities between her newfound joy and ours here on Maui were amazing. Corrie wrote:

> The Lord Jesus has first place in this house. He has given us much important work to do here, and it is because we are doing His will that He blesses the home. Apart from the writing of books and the making of films there is intercession from this house, plus counseling personally and by telephone and letter.[5]

Corrie named her home "Shalom House." The equivalent name in Hawaiian is *Hale Malu*, and that is what this house has been. A house of peace. This brings me back to the beginning when my friend Steph came over and sat with me in the white wicker chairs. She had come to this house of peace hoping for "tea and sympathy." At the time she felt like a victim due to all the circumstances going on in her life that were out of her control. Like Noah's wife she had been going along for the ride, waiting for God to open the door.

After Steph left that afternoon I'd strung together the lei of white plumerias and headed to the airport to meet our incoming guest. As I stood at the arrival gate, my phone rang. It was Steph. The answer about the new job had come. They were moving to the mainland. The waiting and wondering was over. God had opened the door at just the right moment. The big picture was coming into view, and it was clear to see all the ways that God had been providing for her family and protecting them during the journey.

"I've been thinking about what you said," Steph told me. "It may seem like I'm at the mercy of everyone else's decisions, but ultimately God is working out his plan. We really are victims of grace, aren't we?"

---

5 Corrie ten Boom, *Life Lessons from the Hiding Place*, author: Pam Rosewell Moore (Grand Rapids, MI: Chosen Books, 2004), 186.

"Yes, we are." I was still smiling when I hung up and put my phone back in my purse. The first wave of arrivals from the mainland flight streamed through the exit door and made their way to baggage claim. The plumeria lei hung from my forearm, a fragrant live offering ready to be offered as a gift. I watched each face, waiting to see my arriving guest. There she was! I hurried toward her, looping the full circle of flowers around her neck and kissing her with the traditional greeting of aloha.

My eighty-three-year-old mother beamed with delight. She had dreamed of coming to Maui for many years and at last she'd come.

It's never too late to dream a new dream. God was accomplishing his plans for my mother with his usual extravagant kindness and love.

Sliding her cool hand through my bent arm, my mother leaned on me for support. We took the next steps together, two kindred victims of grace, ready to once again see what happens when God's goodness prevails.

> "The things that happen do not happen by chance, they happen entirely in the decree of God. God is working out His purposes.
>
> "If we are in communion with God and recognize that He is taking us into His purposes, we shall no longer try to find out what His purposes are. As we go on in the Christian life it gets simpler, because we are less inclined to say — Now why did God allow this and that? Behind the whole thing lies the compelling of God ... A Christian is one who trusts the wits and the wisdom of God, and not his own wits. If we have a purpose of our own, it destroys the simplicity and the leisureliness which ought to characterize the children of God."[6]

6 Oswald Chambers, *My Utmost for His Highest* (Uhrichsville, Ohio: Barbour Publishing, 1963), August 5.

Brothers and sisters, may the grace of our Lord
Jesus Christ be with your spirit. Amen

— GALATIANS 6:18 NIrV

DISCUSSION QUESTIONS FOR *VICTIM OF GRACE*

Chapter 1 – Free Fall to Full Circle

1. Consider a time when you felt as if you were at the mercy of other people's decisions or a victim of circumstances. Did you sense your faith being tested? In what ways did God comfort or encourage you? Or did the "Teacher" seem silent during the test?

Chapter 2 – The Dream That Would Not Go Away

1. What dream do you have a dream that won't go away?
2. What surprised you the most about this retelling of Hannah's story?
3. As you consider Hannah keeping her promise to give her son back to God, think about the promises you've made over the years. Which ones were the most difficult to keep? What promise are you struggling to keep now? Psalm 15:4 mentions, "Those who … keep their promises even when it hurts" (NLT). How might your life be different moving forward if you keep a promise even when it hurts?

Chapter 3 – Everything is Redeemable

1. In what ways do you struggle with the idea that everything is redeemable?
2. Can you remember times in your life when you were afraid, so you hid and tried to cover up? How did God draw you out of your hiding place? How did you respond to him?

Chapter 4 – A Blessing Inside the Obedience

1. Describe a time in your life when you woke on a morning like any other and yet by the time you put your head on your pillow that night everything had changed. As you look back, what were some of the small steps that led to that big moment of change?
2. What part of this passage from page 60 best describes your current attitude toward God: "It's as if we take credit for the passion that has long brewed inside us, usurping the position of Director of Dreams and demanding favors from God. Or worse, we allow the wickedness of entitlement to seep in, believing we deserve whatever we want because God owes us. In our prayers, we become brassy adolescents, pointing our fingers at God and demanding that he make good on his promises."
3. What hard work of the daily, mundane acts of service do you need to do as you wait for God to move in his way and in his time?

Chapter 5 - Making Peace with the Mysteries

1. What mystery about life would you ask God to explain if you could?

2. Mary in Latvia didn't find God's plans for her life thwarted in spite of her physical limitations. In what ways have you been thinking your circumstances limit God? What might change if you saw your circumstances differently?

Chapter 6 – A Banner Word

1. What do you find appealing in the idea of asking God to give you a word for the year? What might concern you about such an idea?
2. How could you fit "selah" days into your busy schedule? Is there a place you would like to spend time to "pause and ponder"?
3. Can you relate to Robin's description of feeling "tormented" as a result of her inability to forgive? If there are people you haven't forgiven, what is stopping you from doing that right now?
4. What did you see in the story of Lazarus, Mary, and Martha that you hadn't seen before?

Chapter 7 – The Day My Daddy Winked at Me

1. What are your memories of 9/11? Did you or someone in your family reach out to mend a torn relationship as a result of that tragedy?
2. In what ways can you relate to Leah's determined efforts to win Jacob's affection and to change her circumstances? What behavior and mindset would you need to change that would enable you to stop striving?
3. Can you recall a time you changed even though your circumstances didn't?

Chapter 8 – Pure Grace in Every Season

1. Which season in God's creation is your favorite?
2. Which season of the heart are you in right now?
3. What does accepting "the anxiety of feeling yourself in suspense and incomplete" look like in your life right now? Does the restlessness cause you to trust God more or to become more anxious?
4. Robin's opening line in her novel *Gardenias for Breakfast* is, "Everybody has a story. You listen to their story, honey girl, and your story will come and find you." When has listening to someone else resulted in your story making sense to you?

Chapter 9 – Dare to Dream Again

1. In Genesis 12:2 God told Abraham, "I will bless you, and you will be a blessing." In what ways has God blessed you? In what ways can you be a blessing to others as a result?
2. Ruth managed to navigate her way through her relationship with Naomi even though Naomi had become bitter and declared her emptiness to others. How have you navigated your way through relationships with others who have toxic attitudes?
3. Imagine for a moment what might have happened if, instead of staying on the threshing floor and waiting for Boaz, Ruth had given way to insecurity and doubt and fled. What would have changed not only in her life but also in history? How might your family legacy be changed if you put all your hope in God the way Ruth did?

Chapter 10 – Hi. God Likes You a Lot!

1. How did this chapter change your thinking about Mary?
2. What situation do you need to switch your thinking about from "How can this be?" to "How will this be?"
3. What needs to change in your thought processes so you decide to "show up" the next time an unexpected opportunity arises?

Chapter 11 – Going Home

1. Robin described what it was like to finally wash clothes in Africa. What "bucket moment" do you recall when you discovered a dream you had pined for wasn't what you thought it would be? How did your bucket moment change the next step in your life?
2. When would you have been better off responding as Noah's wife did and saying nothing? How does it settle inside you when you think about going along for the ride in the floating ark of your life?
3. After considering the stories in this book and taking a closer look at these kindred victims of grace from Scripture, what principles have you learned that help you to say you are a victim of grace rather than a victim of circumstances?

katie weldon series

Peculiar Treasures

Robin Jones Gunn

Bestselling Author of the Christy Miller Series

On a Whim

Robin Jones Gunn

Bestselling Author of the Christy Miller Series

Available in stores and online!
Also available as an ebook.

Novels by Robin Jones Gunn

Under a Maui Moon
Canary Island Song
Cottage by the Sea
Love Finds You in Sunset Beach, Hawaii

Sisterchick® Novels

Sisterchicks on the Loose
Sisterchicks Do the Hula
Sisterchicks in Sombreros
Sisterchicks Down Under
Sisterchicks Say Ooh La La
Sisterchicks Go Brit
Sisterchicks in Wooden Shoes
Take Flight! A Sisterchicks Devotional

The Glenbrooke Series

Secrets
Whispers
Echoes
Sunsets
Clouds
Waterfalls
Woodlands
Wildflowers

Young Adult Novels

The Christy Miller Series
The Sierra Jensen Series
The College Years
The Katie Weldon Series

For more details on Robin Jones Gunn
or to subscribe to the Robin's Nest Newsletter
or find out about her speaking events,
please visit her website: www.robingunn.com